WALKS IN THE
LOIRE
VALLEY

Titles in the Footpaths of Europe Series

Normandy and the Seine
Walking through Brittany
Walks in Provence
Coastal Walks: Normandy and Brittany
Walking the Pyrenees
Walks in the Auvergne
Walks in the Dordogne
Walks in the Loire Valley
Walking the GR5: Modane to Larche
Walking the GR5: Lake Geneva to Mont-Blanc
Paris to Boulogne
Walks in Corsica

The publishers thank the following people for permission to use their photographs in this book: J. Cantaloube, H. Viaux, J. M. Humeau, D. Fortunato.

WALKS IN THE LOIRE VALLEY

Translated by Andrew Wilson
in association with First Edition

Robertson McCarta

The publishers thank the following people for their help with this book: Isabelle
Daguin, Philippe Lambert, Serge Sineux, Daphne Terry

First published in 1990 by

Robertson McCarta Limited
122 King's Cross Road,
London WC1X 9DS

in association with

Fédération Française de Randonnée Pédestre
8 Avenue Marceau
75008 Paris

© Robertson McCarta Limited
© Fédération Française de Randonnée Pédestre
© Maps, Institut Geographique National (French Official Survey)
    and Robertson McCarta Limited.

Managing Editor Folly Marland
Series designed by Prue Bucknall
Production by Grahame Griffiths
Typeset by Columns Limited, Reading
Planning Map by Rodney Paull

Printed and bound in Spain by Graficas Estella S.A.

British Library Cataloguing in Publication Data

Walks in the Loire — (Footpaths of Europe)
    1. France. Loire Valley – Visitors' guides
    I. Series
    914.4'504838

    ISBN 1–85365–194–X

CONTENTS

IGN map legend	6
A note from the publisher	7
Key	8
The footpaths of France, introduction by Robin Neillands	9
Walks in the Loire valley, introduction	15

The walks and maps

Walk 1 23

GR32 Malesherbes ▶ Pithiviers ▶ Orléans

Walk 2 51

GR3 Orléans ▶ Beaugency ▶ Blois ▶
Chaumont ▶ Amboise ▶ Montlouis ▶ Tours ▶
Artannes ▶ Chinon ▶ Fontevraud ▶ Saumur

Walk 3 109

GR3 Saumur ▶ Trèves
GR3 Trèves ▶ Gennes ▶ La-Haie-Longue
GR3D Alternative route: Trèves ▶ Thouarce ▶ La-Haie-Longue
GR3 La-Haie-Longue ▶ Challones ▶ Saint-Florent ▶
Champtoceaux ▶ Nantes ▶ Orvault ▶ Savenay ▶
La Norielle
GR3 La Norielle ▶ Le Rocher ▶ Les Métairies
Bois-Joubert Alternative route: La Norielle ▶
La Sencie ▶ Domaine de Bois-Joubert ▶ Les Métairies
GR3 Les Métairies ▶ Guérande

Accommodation guide	199
Index	203

Key to IGN Maps

Motorway, dual carriageway

Major road, four lanes or more

Main road, two-lane or three-lane, wide

Main road, two-lane, narrow

Narrow road, regularly surfaced

Other narrow road: regularly surfaced; irregularly surfaced

Possibly private or controlled access

Field track, forest track, felling track, footpath

Track of disused road. Road under construction

Road through embankment, cutting. Tree-lined road or track

Bank. Hedge, line of trees

Railway: double track, single track. Electrified line. Station, waiting line. Halt, stop

Sidings or access lines. Narrow gauge line. Rack railway

Electricity transmission line. Cable railway. Ski lift

National boundary with markers

Boundary and administrative centre of department, district — PF · SP

Boundary and administrative centre of canton, commune — CT · C

For shooting times, go to town hall or gendarmerie

Boundary of military camp, firing range

Boundary of State forest, National Park; outer zone of National Park

Triangulation points

Church, chapel, shrine. Cross, tomb, religious statue. Cemetery

Watch tower, fortress. Windmill, wind-pump. Chimney — Tr · Chem.

Storage tank: oil, gas. Blast furnace. Pylon. Quarry

Cave. Monument, pillar. Castle. Ruins — Mon.

Megalithic monument: dolmen, menhir. Viewpoint. Campsite — P.V.

Market-hall, shed, glasshouse, casemate

Access to underground workings. Refuge. Ski-jump — Mine · Cave

Population/thousands — 183,2   0,4   0,15   0,06

Bridge. Footbridge. Ford. Ferry

Lake, pool. Area liable to flooding. Marsh

Source, spring. Well, water-tank. Water-tower, reservoir — Ch⁰ᵘ d'Eau

Watercourse lined with trees. Waterfall. Dam. Dyke

Navigable canal, feeder or irrigator. Lock, machine-operated. Underground channel

Contour lines. 10 m. interval. Hollow. Small basin. Scree

Principal

Secondary

Woodland   Scrub   Orchard, plantation   Vines   Ricefield

All maps are IGN Orange series. 1:50 000

A note from the publisher

The books in this French Walking Guide series are published in association and with the help of the Fédération Française de la Randonnée Pédestre (French ramblers' association) — generally known as the FFRP.

The FFRP is a federal organisation and is made up of regional, local and many other associations and bodies that form its constituent parts. Individual membership is through these various local organisations. The FFRP therefore acts as an umbrella organisation overseeing the waymarking of footpaths, training and the publishing of the Topoguides, detailed guides to the Grande Randonnée footpaths.

There are at present about 170 Topoguides in print, compiled and written by local members of the FFRP, who are responsible for waymarking the walks — so they are well researched and accurate.

We have translated the main itinerary descriptions, amalgamating and adapting several Topoguides to create new regional guides. We have retained the basic Topoguide structure, indicating length and times of walks, and the Institut Géographique National (official French survey) maps overlaid with the routes.

The information contained in this guide is the latest available at the time of going to print. However, as publishers we are aware that this kind of information is continually changing and we are anxious to enhance and improve the guides as much as possible. We encourage you to send us suggestions, criticisms and those little bits of information you may wish to share with your fellow walkers. Our address is: Robertson-McCarta, 122 King's Cross Road, London WC1X 9DS.

We shall be happy to offer a free copy of any one of these books to any reader whose suggestions are subsequently incorporated into a new edition.

It is possible to create a variety of routes by referring to the walks in the Contents page and to the planning map (inside the front cover). Transport is listed in the alphabetical index in the back of the book and there is an accommodation guide.

KEY

Gournay

This example shows that it is 7km from Gournay to Arbois, and that you can expect it to take 2 hours, 10 minutes.

7Km
2:10

ARBOIS
14th century church

Arbois has a variety of facilities, including hotels and buses. Hotel addresses and bus/train connections may be listed in the index at the back of the book.

a grey arrow indicates an alternative route that leaves and returns to the main route.

Detour

indicates a short detour off the route to a town with facilities or to an interesting sight.

Symbols:

hotel;
youth hostel, hut or refuge;
camping;
restaurant;
cafe;

shops;
railway station;
buses;
ferry;
tourist information.

THE FOOTPATHS OF FRANCE

by Robin Neillands

Why should you go walking in France? Well, walking is fun and as for France, Danton summed up the attractions of that country with one telling phrase: 'Every man has two countries,' he said, 'his own . . . and France.' That is certainly true in my case and I therefore consider it both a pleasure and an honour to write this general introduction to these footpath guides to France. A pleasure because walking in or through France is my favourite pastime, an honour because these excellent English language guides follow in the course set by those Topo-guides published in French by the Fédération Française pour la Randonnée Pédestre, which set a benchmark for quality that all footpath guides might follow. Besides, I believe that good things should be shared and walking in France is one of the most pleasant activities I know.

I have been walking in France for over thirty years. I began by rambling — or rather ambling — through the foothills of the Pyrenees, crossing over into Spain past the old Hospice de France, coming back over the Somport Pass in a howling blizzard, which may account for the fact that I totally missed two sets of frontier guards on both occasions. Since then I have walked in many parts of France and even from one end of it to the other, from the Channel to the Camargue, and I hope to go on walking there for many years to come.

The attractions of France are legion, but there is no finer way to see and enjoy them than on foot. France has two coasts, at least three mountain ranges — the Alps, Pyrenees and the Massif Central — an agreeable climate, a great sense of space, good food, fine wines and, believe it or not, a friendly and hospitable people. If you don't believe me, go there on foot and see for yourself. Walking in France will appeal to every kind of walker, from the day rambler to the backpacker, because above all, and in the nicest possible way, the walking in France is well organised, but those Francophiles who already know France well, will find it even more pleasureable if they explore their favourite country on foot.

The GR system

The Grande Randonnée (GR) footpath network now consists of more than 40,000 kilometres (25,000 miles) of long-distance footpath, stretching into every part of France, forming a great sweep around Paris, probing deeply into the Alps, the Pyrenees, and the volcanic cones of the Massif Central. This network, the finest system of footpaths in Europe, is the creation of that marvellously named organisation, *la Fédération Française de Randonnée Pédestre, Comité National des Sentiers de Grande Randonnée*, which I shall abbreviate to FFRP-CNSGR. Founded in 1948, and declaring that, *'un jour de marche, huit jours de santé,'* the FFRP-CNSGR has flourished for four decades and put up the now familiar red-and-white waymarks in every corner of the country. Some of these footpaths are classic walks, like the famous GR65, *Le Chemin de St Jacques*, the ancient Pilgrim Road to Compostela, the TMB, the *Tour du Mont Blanc*, which circles the mountain through France, Switzerland and Italy, or the 600-mile long GR3, the *Sentier de la Loire*, which runs from the Ardèche to the Atlantic, to give three examples from the hundred or so GR trails available. In addition there is an abundance of GR du Pays or regional footpaths, like the *Sentier de la Haute Auvergne*, and the *Sentier Tour des Monts d'Aubrac*. A 'Tour' incidentally, is usually a circular walk. Many of these regional or provincial GR trails are charted and waymarked in red-

and-yellow by local outdoor organisations such as ABRI (Association Bretonne des Relais et Itineraires) for Brittany, or CHAMINA for the Massif Central. The walker in France will soon become familiar with all these footpath networks, national, regional or local, and find them the perfect way into the heart and heartland of France. As a little bonus, the GR networks are expanding all the time, with the detours — or *varientes* — off the main route eventually linking with other GR paths or *varientes* and becoming GR trails in their own right.

Walkers will find the GR trails generally well marked and easy to follow, and they have two advantages over the footpaths commonly encountered in the UK. First, since they are laid out by local people, they are based on intricate local knowledge of the local sights. If there is a fine view, a mighty castle or a pretty village on your footpath route, your footpath through France will surely lead you to it. Secondly, all French footpaths are usually well provided with a wide range of comfortable country accommodation, and you will discover that the local people, even the farmers, are well used to walkers and greet them with a smile, a '*Bonjour*' and a '*bon route*'.

Terrain and climate

As a glance at these guides or any Topo-guide will indicate, France has a great variety of terrain. France is twice the size of the UK and many natural features are also on a larger scale. There are three main ranges of mountains: the Alps contain the highest mountain in Europe, the Pyrenees go up to 10,000 ft, the Massif Central peaks to over 6000 ft, and there are many similar ranges with hills which overtop our highest British peak, Ben Nevis. On the other hand, the Auvergne and the Jura have marvellous open ridge walking, the Cévennes are steep and rugged, the Ardèche and parts of Provence are hot and wild, the Île de France, Normandy, Brittany and much of Western France is green and pleasant, not given to extremes. There is walking in France for every kind of walker, but given such a choice the wise walker will consider the complications of terrain and weather before setting out, and go suitably equipped.

France enjoys three types of climate: continental, oceanic and mediterranean. South of the Loire it will certainly be hot to very hot from mid-April to late September. Snow can fall on the mountains above 4,000 ft from mid-October and last until May, or even lie year-round on the tops and in couloirs; in the high hills an ice-axe is never a frill. I have used one by the Brêche de Roland in the Pyrenees in mid-June.

Wise walkers should study weather maps and forecasts carefully in the week before they leave for France, but can generally expect good weather from May to October, and a wide variety of weather — the severity depending on the terrain — from mid-October to the late Spring.

Accommodation

The walker in France can choose from a wide variety of accommodation with the assurance that the walker will always be welcome. This can range from country hotels to wild mountain pitches, but to stay in comfort, many walkers will travel light and overnight in the comfortable hotels of the *Logis de France* network.

Logis de France: The *Logis de France* is a nationwide network of small, family-run country hotels, offering comfortable accommodation and excellent food. *Logis* hotels are graded and can vary from a simple, one-star establishment, with showers and linoleum, to a four- or five-star *logis* with gastronomic menus and deep-pile carpets. All offer excellent value for money, and since there are over 5,000 scattered across the French countryside, they provide a good focus for a walking day. An annual guide to the *Logis* is available from the French Government Tourist Office, 178 Piccadilly, London W1V 0AL, Tel. (01) 491 7622.

Gîtes d'étape: A *gîte d'étape* is best imagined as an unmanned youth hostel for outdoor folk of all ages. They lie all along the footpath networks and are usually signposted or listed in the guides. They can be very comfortable, with bunk beds, showers, a well equipped kitchen, and in some cases they have a warden, a *guardien*, who may offer meals. *Gîtes d'étape* are designed exclusively for walkers, climbers, cyclists, cross country skiers or horse-riders. A typical price (1990) would be Fr.25 for one night. *Gîtes d'étape* should not be confused with a *Gîte de France*. A *gîte* — usually signposted as '*Gîte de France*' — is a country cottage available for a holiday let, though here too, the owner may be more than willing to rent it out as overnight accommodation.

Youth hostels: Curiously enough, there are very few Youth Hostels in France outside the main towns. A full list of the 200 or so available can be obtained from the Youth Hostel Association (YHA), Trevelyan House, St Albans, Herts AL1 2DY.

Pensions or cafes: In the absence of an hotel, a *gîte d'étape* or a youth hostel, all is not lost. France has plenty of accommodation and an enquiry at the village cafe or bar will usually produce a room. The cafe/hotel may have rooms or suggest a nearby pension or a *chambre d'hôte*. Prices start at around Fr.50 for a room, rising to, say, Fr.120. (1990 estimate).

Chambres d'hôte: A *chambre d'hôte* is a guest room or, in English terms, a bed-and-breakfast, usually in a private house. Prices range up from about Fr.60 a night. *Chambres d'hôte* signs are now proliferating in the small villages of France and especially if you can speak a little French are an excellent way to meet the local people. Prices (1990) are from, say, Fr.70 a night for a room, not per person.

Abris: *Abris*, shelters or mountain huts can be found in the mountain regions, where they are often run by the *Club Alpin Français*, an association for climbers. They range from the comfortable to the primitive, are often crowded and are sometimes reserved for members. Details from the Club Alpin Français, 7 Rue la Boétie, Paris 75008, France.

Camping: French camp sites are graded from one to five star, but are generally very good at every level, although the facilities naturally vary from one cold tap to shops, bars and heated pools. Walkers should not be deterred by a '*Complet*' (Full) sign on the gate or office window: a walker's small tent will usually fit in somewhere. *Camping à la ferme*, or farm camping, is increasingly popular, more primitive — or less regimented — than the official sites, but widely available and perfectly adequate. Wild camping is officially not permitted in National Parks, but unofficially if you are over 1,500m away from a road, one hour's walk from a *gîte* or campsite, and where possible ask permission, you should have no trouble. French country people will always assist the walker to find a pitch.

The law for walkers

The country people of France seem a good deal less concerned about their 'rights' than the average English farmer or landowner. I have never been ordered off land in

11

France or greeted with anything other than friendliness . . . maybe I've been lucky. As a rule, walkers in France are free to roam over all open paths and tracks. No decent walker will leave gates open, trample crops or break down walls, and taking fruit from gardens or orchards is simply stealing. In some parts of France there are local laws about taking chestnuts, mushrooms (and snails), because these are cash crops. Signs like *Réserve de Chasse*, or *Chasse Privé* indicate that the shooting is reserved for the landowner. As a general rule, behave sensibly and you will be tolerated everywhere, even on private land.

The country code

Walkers in France should obey the *Code du Randonneur*:

- Love and respect Nature.
- Avoid unnecessary noise.
- Destroy nothing.
- Do not leave litter.
- Do not pick flowers or plants.
- Do not disturb wildlife.
- Re-close all gates.
- Protect and preserve the habitat.
- No smoking or fires in the forests. (This rule is essential and is actively enforced by foresters and police.)
- Stay on the footpath.
- Respect and understand the country way of life and the country people.
- Think of others as you think of yourself.

Transport

Transportation to and within France is generally excellent. There are no less than nine Channel ports: Dunkirk, Calais, Boulogne, Dieppe, Le Havre, Caen/Ouistreham, Cherbourg, Saint-Malo and Roscoff, and a surprising number of airports served by direct flights from the UK. Although some of the services are seasonal, it is often possible to fly direct to Toulouse, Poitiers, Nantes, Perpignan, Montpellier, indeed to many provincial cities, as well as to Paris and such obvious destinations as Lyon and Nice. Within France the national railway, the SNCF, still retains a nationwide network. Information, tickets and a map can be obtained from the SNCF. France also has a good country bus service and the *gare routière* is often placed just beside the railway station. Be aware though, that many French bus services only operate within the *département*, and they do not generally operate from one provincial city to the next. I cannot encourage people to hitch-hike, which is both illegal and risky, but walkers might consider a taxi for their luggage. Almost every French village has a taxi driver who will happily transport your rucksacks to the next night-stop, fifteen to twenty miles away, for Fr.50 a head or even less.

Money

Walking in France is cheap, but banks are not common in the smaller villages, so carry a certain amount of French money and the rest in traveller's cheques or Eurocheques, which are accepted everywhere.

Clothing and equipment

The amount of clothing and equipment you will need depends on the terrain, the length of the walk, the time of your visit, the accommodation used. Outside the mountain areas it is not necessary to take the full range of camping or backpacking gear. I once walked across France from the Channel to the Camargue along the Grande Randonnée footpaths in March, April and early May and never needed to use any of the camping gear I carried in my rucksack because I found hotels everywhere, even in quite small villages.

Essential items are:
In summer: light boots, a hat, shorts, suncream, lip salve, mosquito repellent, sunglasses, a sweater, a windproof cagoule, a small first-aid kit, a walking stick.
In winter: a change of clothing, stormproof outer garments, gaiters, hat, lip salve, a companion.
In the mountains at any time: large-scale maps (1:25,000), a compass, an ice-axe. In winter, add a companion and ten-point crampons.
At any time: a phrase book, suitable maps, a dictionary, a sense of humour.

The best guide to what to take lies in the likely weather and the terrain. France tends to be informal, so there is no need to carry a jacket or something smart for the evenings. I swear by Rohan clothing, which is light, smart and functional. The three things I would never go without are light, well-broken-in boots and several pairs of loop-stitched socks, and my walking stick.

Health hazards
Health hazards are few. France can be hot in summer, so take a full water-bottle and refill it at every opportunity. A small first-aid kit is sensible, with plasters and 'mole-skin' for blisters, but since prevention is better than cure, loop-stitched socks and flexible boots are better. Any French chemist — a *pharmacie* — is obliged to render first-aid treatment for a small fee. These pharmacies can be found in most villages and large towns and are marked by a green cross.

Dogs are both a nuisance and a hazard. All walkers in France should carry a walking stick to fend off aggressive curs. Rabies — *la rage* — is endemic and anyone bitten must seek immediate medical advice. France also possesses two types of viper, which are common in the hill areas of the south. In fairness, although I found my walking stick indispensable, I must add that in thirty years I have never even seen a snake or a rabid dog. In case of real difficulty, dial 17 for the police and the ambulance.

Food and wine
One of the great advantages with walking in France is that you can end the day with a good meal and not gain an ounce. French country cooking is generally excellent and good value for money, with the price of a four-course menu starting at about Fr 45. The ingredients for the mid-day picnic can be purchased from the village shops and these also sell wine. Camping-Gaz cylinders and cartridges are widely available, as is 2-star petrol for stoves. Avoid naked fires.

Preparation
The secret of a good walk lies in making adequate preparations before you set out. It pays to be fit enough to do the daily distance at the start. Much of the necessary information is contained in this guide, but if you need more, look in guidebooks or outdoor magazines, or ask friends.

The French

I cannot close this introduction without saying a few words about the French, not least because the walker in France is going to meet rather more French people than, say, a motorist will, and may even meet French people who have never met a foreigner before. It does help if the visitor speaks a little French, even if only enough to say '*bonjour*' and '*Merci*' and '*S'il vous plaît*'. The French tend to be formal and it pays to be polite, to say 'hello', to shake hands. I am well aware that relations between France and England have not always been cordial over the last six hundred years or so, but I have never met with hostility of any kind in thirty years of walking through France. Indeed, I have always found that if the visitor is prepared to meet the French halfway, they will come more than halfway to greet him or her in return, and are both friendly and hospitable to the passing stranger.

As a final tip, try smiling. Even in France, or especially in France, a smile and a '*pouvez vous m'aider?*' (Can you help me?) will work wonders. That's my last bit of advice, and all I need do now is wish you '*Bonne Route*' and good walking in France.

WALKS IN THE LOIRE VALLEY

The difference between a motorist and a walker is that a motorist passes through and a walker bonds, step by step, through his five senses — hearing, sight, taste, touch and smell — with the region he explores. And there is no better place to appreciate this than treading the footpaths of the Loire Valley, long renowned for the subtle variations of its fascinating landscape, its superb châteaux, splendid vineyards and wonderful food.

The Loire itself is the longest river in France. It begins its journey high up in the Cevennes mountains, embarking on a route north to Orléans, then west to Nantes and the Atlantic Ocean. It flows through a dozen *departements* of lush green, peaceful countryside, passing by ancient towns and imposing châteaux. It has thriving vineyards planted along both of its banks, and the region's gentle climate, luminosity, views, fertile valleys, sedate villages, châteaux and history make it a very special area to explore on foot.

Listed among the valley's many historical celebrities are Henry II and Richard Coeur de Lion; and the English and French played what has been described as 'hot potato' with the region until Joan of Arc helped win it for the French during the Hundred Years' War.

The area is renowned for its light white wines, muscadets and champagnes, and nearly every town has a local wine well worth resting a while to sample! Regional delicacies and specialities, such as *rillettes* abound and make perfect accompaniments to the wine.

THE WALKS
Malesherbes to Orléans
The 90 kilometres of GR32 link two of the oldest French provinces, the Ile de France and the Orléanais, and two of the oldest long-distance footpaths, GR1, which encircles the Paris region, and GR3, the Loire footpath. The route is divided into four main sections. The first takes the rambler through the fresh green upper valley of the Essonne as it cuts its way through the limestone of the Beauce. The walk follows the river upstream from mill to mill, from Buthier, close to Malesherbes, to the area around its source — a distance of about 50 kilometres. The second section crosses the Orléans State forest, from north to south, over a distance of 15 kilometres. This area contains the first junction with the GR3 and takes the hiker from the basin of the Seine to that of the Loire.

The third section follows the Orléans canal which was dug in the 17th century in the former valley of the Cens or Oussance. The fourth section follows the banks of the Loire into the heart of Orléans, where the GR3 meets the GR32 for the last time.

The rich and varied landscape is matched by the regional differences of the many villages through which the walker passes on the way through the valley of Essonne, across the forest of Orléans and down the Loire Valley. Ramblers will delight in this splendid route, which is not physically taxing and where the climate is temperate all year through.

Orléans to Saumur

Doubtless because of the fertility of its valleys, the Touraine has been described as 'the garden of France'. It is equally well known for its many imposing châteaux, and a walk through the Touraine is a journey back through history. This wine-growing area around Tours dates back to Roman times, as does the town itself. As early as the 6th century, Tours was a place of pilgrimage and, in the 15th and 16th centuries, it was famous for its silk production. The attractive rolling landscape is flatter around Tours itself and hillier in the hinterland. The vines are planted on the gently undulating slopes, which are often south facing. It is renowned for its rich variety of wines.

Balzac said of the area: 'I love the Touraine as an artist loves art'. After the Middle Ages, and the flowering of Romanesque abbeys and churches, the Renaissance burst forth in the Loire Valley, leaving in its wake a delicate stone tracery of châteaux. Amidst such magnificence it is very to easy to imagine the presence of kings. It was at Chenonceaux that a very young man was walking one day, deep in reverie. His name was Jean-Jacques Rousseau, and he had already started to write the 'Reveries of a solitary walker'. The best way to become acquainted with this fascinating region is to ramble along its winding paths which climb steeply and rush downwards like toboggans. Take time to idle, walking past old troglodyte caves, around old farms and along paths that wind through vineyards.

An encounter with the Loire at Beaugency means a memorable visit to the enormous Keep, the Tour de Cesar, and the magnificent bridge that spans the river. You will not forget the streets decorated with flowers in a canalized watercourse bordered by ivy-leaved geraniums; and the infinite patience etched on the faces of the women of old, whose head-dresses, finished in straw, can be seen in the regional museum.

Very close to here, at Meung-sur-Loire, Jehan de Meung completed the 'Roman de la Rose' begun by Guillaume de Lorris, a native of the forest of Orléans. 'Without me, none of the joys of life can exist' — this is, of course, part of a hymn to wine, written in Orléans in the 13th century.

The Loiret was once covered in vineyards, but only the best now remain. These include the vineyards of Baule, between Meung and Beaugency, the *gris-meunier* and *auvergnat* of Mareaux-aux-Pres and the wines of Ousson-sur-Loire on the edge of the slopes of the Giennois. As in all areas where vines are cultivated, the people are friendler and more welcoming than usual.

If A. Chavaud, a pharmacist of Orléans is to be believed, the wines of Orléans are 'as light as an evening breeze, as vivid as lightening, as endearing as a page boy, as elegant as a maiden and as fresh as a summer's rose'.

Orléans is also famous for its old-fashioned vinegar, and a small factory, the house of Martin-Pouret, continues to produce this renowned product, which originated because, in earlier times, wine that was shipped up the Loire and unloaded at Orléans, was sometimes kept for too long on the wharves, where it turned to vinegar!

Above all else, the Touraine is the River Loire which, in all its splendour, flows under a great expanse of sky between fertile meadows and white sandbanks — the Loire of painters, poets, writers, and builders of cathedrals, churches and châteaux.

Saumur to Guérande

Saumur, situated as it is within the borders of the Anjou appellation is known as the Pearl of Anjou.

From Saumur onwards, as the GR3 crosses Maine-et-Loire, the footpath turns away from the river on only three occasions. Two of the detours take you along the hillside to a wooden region where you pass megaliths and troglodytic dwellings. The third detour, north of Mauges, avoids the monotony of a straight flat route.

These detours aside, the footpath follows its tranquil route along the royal river as the walker proceeds at a steady pace from the Paris Basin to the Massif Armoricain.

As you leave the Saumur district for the area around Saint-Saturnin, the fields are bordered by slate walls. At Juigné-sur-Loire, there is a château with walls of schist. Beyond Angers, the Loire widens. The GR3 crosses the Pays Nantais from east to west, as does the Loire. From Ingrandes, for a distance of about 35 kilometres, the river marks the boundary between the Loire-Atlantique and the Maine-et-Loire, or, in other words, the province of Anjou.

Here upstream of Champtoceaux, the last but one village in Anjou, the GR3 reaches a section where the valley is both narrow and sharply delineated as it runs between the wide Ancensis basin and the beginning of the Val Nantais, where the valley opens out as the river approaches the sea. The characteristic sight of the many arms of the great river flowing between wooded islands and white sandbanks merges with the picturesque Breton countryside, where vineyards and market gardening temper the austerity of the slopes of dark schist. Although some of these slopes are quite steep, they never exceed a height of 80 metres. Around and throughout the entire Pays Nantais, there are low plateaux formed of Cambrian or pre-Cambrian crystalline schists. Where it comes to the surface, the rock is sometimes a fragile mica-schist, which crumbles in the hand.

This is ancient country, often laid down more than 600 and never less than 300 million years ago, and levelled down to form a peneplain. This is done in such a way that horizontal lines dominate the far reaches of the landscape. Weathered by thousands of millennia of sun and rain these plateaux are covered with a thick mantle of compact clay with mica. This is responsible for a certain softness, and causes the notorious mud that, in winter, turns so many country footpaths into quagmires.

Château de Cheverny

The agricultural landscape on these plateaux is largely bocage (hedgeland: little fields and meadows divided by hedges). Villages crown convex hilltops. There is a sprinkling of isolated farms, and, in the centre of the enormous communes, the market towns crowd round their churches, usually about 150 years old.

At the beginning of the 19th century unprofitable land was developed for agricultural use by the establishment of a geometrical pattern of very large fields (up to six to eight hectares in area), separated by bocage and virtually devoid of habitation. The GR3 crosses this kind of area between Le Cellier and St-Mars, and between Sautron and St-Etienne. The outcrops of lighter soils, generally in areas where the bedrock is granite, were developed in the 13th to 14th centuries by small peasant communities.

Thus the harmony and natural beauty of the landscape is made up of subtle alliances between the rock, the relief, the vegetation, and man's influence on the land. It is interesting to note that, in this countryside, where the rustling of trees and vegetation is everywhere, there are no forests — this is a characteristic of western France. The Pays Nantais has 40,000 hectares of marshes — 'wetlands' — the most famous of which are Grand Lieu and la Brière. The GR3 will take you round the edge of the peaty depression of le petit Mars upstream of Sucé, and, in particular, will give you a fine view of the estuary marshlands from the top of the 'Sillon de Bretagne'. In order to appreciate the origins of these marshlands you will need to imagine a time 50,000 years ago when the Atlantic was a good 100 metres lower, the shore was a long way from its current position and the Loire flowed vigorously through a deep valley a long way to the south of what now seems to be an alluvial plain (50 metres below sea level at Saint-Nazaire). Ten thousand years ago the sea rushed in to invade the estuary, pushing its briny waters as far as le petit Mars close to the River Erdre, which was soon driven back by the silt which continued to accumulate until the Middle Ages.

The marshlands are an area of dense grass or reeds in summer and immense sheets of silver in winter. They are magnificent on a spring evening when, at the foot of the 'Sillon de Bretagne', they come between you and the setting sun. The exploitation of the marshlands by peasant farmers is a technical miracle, and the salt marshes of the Guérande peninsula are a coastal version of the same phenomenon.

The route followed by the GR3 is a wonderful way to become acquainted with the charm and variety of the Pays Nantais. It will take you round the marshlands of la Brière as far as the medieval city of Guérande.

THE BRIÈRE REGIONAL PARK

The Brière Regional Park covers an area of 40,000 hectares. Situated north of Saint-Nazaire, between the estuary of the Loire and the Vilaine, this region, which constitutes the hinterland of the Côte d'Amour and the salt marshes of the Guérande peninsula, includes the marshlands of la Grande Brière, a single estate of 7,000 hectares which has remained in the joint ownership of the inhabitants of la Brière — a privilege that was officially recognized for the first time on 8 August 1461 by the letters patent of François II, the Duke of Brittany.

The inhabitants of la Brière continue to own and administer their marshland estate, which in some respects constitutes a state within a state. A syndic appointed by each of the 21 communes in the area has sole responsibility for managing the jointly owned estate.

The Brière Regional Park, which covers all or part of the territory of the communes of Assérac, le Baule, la Chapelle-des-Marai, Crossac, Guérande, Herbignac, Missillac, Montoir-de-Bretagne, Pornichet, Saint-André-des-Eaux, Saint-Joachim, Saint-Lyphard, Saint-Malo-de-Guersac, Saint-Nazaire, Sainte-Reine-de-Bretagne and Trignac, is administered by a combined syndicate which includes, in addition to the above-mentioned communes, representatives of the EPR of the Pays de Loire, the department of Loire-Atlantique, the Saint-Nazaire Chamber of Commerce and Industry, the Chamber of Agriculture of Loire-Atlantique, the Syndical Committee of Grand Brière Mottière, the Syndicate of the Marais de Donges and the City of Nantes.

The activities of the Brière Regional Park can be divided into four categories:

1 Protection and promotion of the environment: assistance in the upkeep of the marshland, creation of a wildlife park in order to keep and display the varieties of birds found in Brière in a natural setting.
2 Promotion and development of an exceptional architectural heritage, taking account of the fact that most of the territory within the parks is classed as a listed site.
3 Accommodation and activities for tourists: establishment of museums, Brière Cottage at Fédrun, Clog-maker's House at la Chapelle-des-Marais, Lock-keeper's House and Warden's House at Rozé en Saint-Malo-de-Guersac, the Village de Kerhinet.
4 Preservation of folk traditions and cultural heritage.

Brière National Park:
180, Ile de Fédrun,
44720 Saint-Joachim.
Tel (40) 45 52 50.

Région des Pays de la Loire

Within close proximity of the GR3, there are warm, welcoming and comfortable places to stay. Most accommodation is in Logis de France country hotels

Loire-Atlantique

and inns. They all provide some special local dishes: le Beurre Blanc Nantais (white butter sauce), le canard au Muscadet (duckling gently cooked in Muscadet Wine), les anguilles de Brière (eels from the Brière Nature Park), les fruits de mer (seafood platter)....

LES VOYAGEURS **
Place du 8 mai
44350 GUÉRANDE
M. SALAUN — Tél: **40.24.90.13**
LOGIS DE FRANCE situated 10 minutes from La Baule, opposite the ramparts of Guérande, the Hotel and Restaurant of LES VOYAGEURS offers a warm welcome. The cuisine is based on fresh seafood. 12 fully equipped rooms. TV and direct telephone line - 230/260 FF (prices 1990)

FRANK-HOTEL **
Route de la Garenne
44700 ORVAULT
Mme BERTHE-BOIS — Tél: **40.63.04.79**
Quiet hotel — wooded park — 30 bedrooms with bath and W.C. —
220 FF (prices 1990)

L'AUBERGE DU CALVAIRE *
6 route de la Brière "Le Calvaire"
44169 PONTCHATEAU
Mme COUVRAND — Tél: **40.01.61.65**
Hotel LOGIS DE FRANCE bordering the Briere Nature Park, in a wooded setting. Mrs COUVRAND provides a family welcome and prepares duckling cooked in Muscadet Wine. 12 bedrooms — 180/250 FF (prices 1990)

AUBERGE DE KERHINET **
44410 SAINT-LYPHARD
M. PEBAY — Tél: **40.61.91.46**
LOGIS DE FRANCE setting in the heart of the Brière Nature Park, in a restored hamlet. The charm of a traditional dwelling. 7 separate cottage bedrooms. 170/200 FF (prices 1990)

AUBERGE DU CHENE VERT **
10 place de l'Hôtel de Ville
44260 SAVENAY
M. BOUDAUD — Tél: **40.56.90.16**
LOGIS DE FRANCE entirely renovated in 1989 situated in a "Station Verte de Vacances" (countryside holiday resort). 20 fully equipped bedrooms — 190/380 FF (prices 1990)

L'OISELLERIE *
12 route du Lac
44260 SAVENAY
M. LANGLOIS — Tél: **40.56.98.78**
Between town and lake, a quiet and comfortable hotel — wooded park.
11 fully equipped bedrooms with direct telephone — 85/175 FF (prices 1990)

You will meet many fascinating sights during your walks through the Loire countryside — the Layon vineyards bordered by country houses and cave dwellings still lived in today. You will find hospitality, rest and good food in these Logis de France hotels or inns.

HOTEL DE FRANCE **
5 rue Nationale
49290 CHALONNES-SUR-LOIRE
M. BOURGET - Tél: **41.78.00.12** - Télex: **722 183**
Hotel LOGIS DE FRANCE — English spoken — walking kits — bike rentals
14 bedrooms — 155/230 FF (prices 1990)

HOTEL DES VOYAGEURS *
Promenade du Champalud
49270 CHAMPTOCEAUX
M. RABU — Tél: **41.83.50.09**
Hotel LOGIS DE FRANCE overlooking the Loire — English spoken —
17 bedrooms —
135/165 FF (prices 1990)

AUX NAULETS D'ANJOU
18 rue Croix de Mission
49350 GENNES
Mme DEMARQUE — Tél: **41.51.81.88**
Quiet hotel-restaurant overlooking the village. Garden, car-park, garage for bikes
English spoken. 20 bedrooms 260 FF (prices 1990).

HOTEL DIANE DE MERIDOR — LE BUSSY **
Quai Philippe de Commines
49730 MONTSOREAU
M. WURFFEL — Tél: **41.51.70.18**
Hotel LOGIS DE FRANCE — Restaurant facing the Loire, local "cuisine": fish from the river — overlooking the Château de Montsoreau from the bedrooms —
Private car-park — garden — walking kits — English spoken
15 bedrooms — 130/265FF (prices 1990)

HOSTELLERIE DE LA GABELLE **
Quai de la Loire
SAINT-FLORENT-LE-VIEIL
M. REDUREAU — Tél: **41.72.50.19**
Hotel LOGIS DE FRANCE — A quiet hotel facing the Loire, in a historical city. The chef prepares gastronomic and regional specialities — car-park — English spoken.
20 bedrooms — 150/250 FF (prices 1990)

LOGI, the regional rambling organisation in charge of the Western Loire footpaths (Pays de la Loire).
Ask for our free regional brochure including accommodation, suggestions on walking, cycling, horse riding, water excursions... in order to give you adventurous ideas.

ONTACT: **LOIRE OCEAN GITES ET ITINERAIRES**
Maison du Tourisme — Place du Commerce
44000 NANTES
Tél: **40.35.62.26** — Télex: **711 211**

WALK 1

In order to make it easier to get on to the GR32, the route begins at Malesherbes, which is located on the GR1.

MALESHERBES

Church of Saint-Martin, dating from 13th and 14th centuries and housing an early 16th century entombment. Château with feudal towers and moat, 16th and 17th century buildings, oubliettes, numerous underground passages, imposing four-storey Norman tithe barn, dovecote with 2,500 compartments, large park. Many French kings since Charles VI have stayed here (private property – open every day except Tuesday). The château de Rouville lies 1 kilometre north of the town; it is 15th century Gothic, restored in the 19th century. Open to visitors; enquiries to the caretaker.

3Km
0:40

Detour
Moulin de Mirebeau
The River Essonne is famous for its beauty. There are innumerable mills along its banks, often at intervals of less than 1 kilometre. Now disused, these have been converted into dwellings and a few of them have retained their millwheels.

Opposite the station, bear slightly to the right and follow the GR1 along the tree-lined Allée de Farcheville which is closed to traffic. Cross the N51 and enter the grounds of the château through the zigzag opening beside the main gate. Follow the main avenue for 800 metres; in front of the obelisk, turn left into a tree-lined avenue which leads into the Rue du Château opposite the church of Saint-Martin. Turn right on to the road to Puiseaux; follow this for 150 metres, past the cemetery, and then take the Rue de la Baignade (view of Malesherbes nestling in the surrounding hills) which leads to the left round the beach to the footbridge over the River Essonne.

Detour see left. On the left there is a footpath along the river that forms part of a walk known as the circuit des Bords de l'Essonne and signposted by the Malesherbes tourist information office. 750 metres along, on the N51, is the moulin de Mirebeau, a working mill. From the mill, you enter the village from the north and join the GR1 which leads towards the château de Rouville.

Cross the footbridge; 400 metres further you will begin to cross the Malesherbes marshland.

23

The Malesherbes marshland

From the 13th century onwards, peat from this marshland was used as fuel by the region's inhabitants.

Today, the site is of great value, both for its unusual landscape and its biological interest.

This marsh, which is what remains of other more extensive marshlands, is said by some to be the origin of the name of *Malesherbes* (from the French *mauvaises herbes*, which means weeds). Others maintain that the village owes its name, which until the 18th century was Soisy-Mâles-Herbes, to the extremely rich flora of the surrounding area, which is well known among botanists.

A winding path leads eastwards over spongy ground to the right of the water purification station to a minor road, at a point opposite the rocks of Buthier; turn right and follow the road for 150 metres past the Café Canard to the first crossroads. The GR1 leads straight on over a wide sandy path towards Auxy and Fontaine-bleau, while the GR32 begins on the right.

Buthiers leisure centre

Leisure centre, open only to clubs and associations, spread over 9 hectares. The grotto of Bourelier, located half-way up the rocks behind the auberge Canard, has a sandy floor. In other grottos in the area there are traces of prehistoric inhabitants. In the same direction as the grotto of Bourelier, there is a narrow path through the forest which is an alternative to the GR1 and avoids the village of Auxy.

The GR32 follows a minor road which runs beside a car park at the entrance to the leisure centre. After 250 metres it joins the Auxy road; cross the road and take a path through the trees (left fork). At the rocks, bear right and walk up the hill. At the top, there is a cross dedicated to Saint John the Baptist.

1.95Km
0:30

Detour *5 mins*
BUTHIERS
✵

Detour see left. On leaving the wood, go down the path on the right, alongside a gravel pit and into the village centre. The path then goes to the church just outside the village.

Cross the D103 and take the Chemin de la Messe, the first part of which is surfaced; it then becomes a dirt track running alongside heathland and fields. After a few undulations on the plateau it leads to the woods and, without changing direction (south-west), descends rapidly through them and finishes after a right-hand bend and 100 metres of surfaced road at the Rue des Lilas. Follow the road to the left for 100 metres until you reach the D410 (junction with the road to Boulancourt).

RONCEVAUX
🏠 🍷

Cross the D410 and bear right to go down the Allée des Tilleuls. This straight walk uses the ballast laid down for a railway that was eventually built not along this route, but 500 metres to the south. As the path crosses the Essonne there is an attractive view of the Touveau mill and its grounds (private property). The walk finishes at the D25 opposite a pine-covered slope known as the 'Fragrant hill'.

Detour
1.5Km   **Pinçon**
0:20

Detour see left. If you follow the D25 to the right for 5 metres you will come to a walk signposted by the Malesherbes tourist information office and known as the *circuit de Pinçon*. 200 metres along on the right it leads to a small village pond. Turn right and walk 100 metres along the D25; down below on the right, you will see the former wash house of Pinçon, now restored.

Turn left along the D25; after the subway underneath the railway, you will come to the hamlet of Trezan.

Trezan
At the end of the 12th century, the château was the home of Ferry V du Donjon, lord of Jouy and Thrézan. His son, Guy du Donjon, had a parish church built in 1215, and one of his sons was Bishop of Orléans. Guillaume du Donjon, another son of Ferry V who was a Cistercian monk, was Prior of Fontainejean, then Bishop of Bourges; he died in 1210 and was canonized in 1218. The two brothers Guy and Guillaume are shown side by side on a

Walk through the hamlet. At the first fork, bear slightly to the left and take the minor road that goes down towards the valley, known as the 'nouveau chemin de la Messe'. After the farms, continue straight on along a wooded footpath (do not descend to the left); the path leads up to an isolated rocky site, surrounded by pines, and then on to a cultivated plateau. Here, after a detour of 2 metres to the right, walk across country in a straight line beside a fence, on the left-hand side, to the first farm (Mailleton farm). Turn right and follow the minor road that joins the D25 after 150 metres. Follow it round to the left and after about 900 metres in the hollow of the second little hill go down towards the valley of the Essonne along the Chemin de Maison Rouge.

tombstone that stands at the rear of the church in Malesherbes.

Just before the entrance to the Maison Rouge farm, skirt the building on the right-hand side along a dirt track. Running closer and closer to the Essonne, the track reaches the old Beaudon mill, (which was once a farm, and has now been converted). A small stone bridge crosses the Essonne; then a fishermen's path leads to a restored wash house. At this point, turn away from the river and walk towards some houses (the path is more or less visible across the meadows) and walk along the Allée du moulin Foulon to Pierre Longue where there is a caravan and camping site.

4.85Km
1:15

Cross the road and take a path that climbs up the hillside. It continues in the same direction (north-east), but it becomes grassy and leads through a clearing and small wood before becoming a dirt track, between cultivated fields, that leads diagonally to two towers flanking a gate. Go through the gate and walk down the Promenade des Tours, where there are meadows, pine trees, junipers and recreation areas with benches, to Boulancourt.

BOULANCOURT
Ⓐ ✕ ♆ ⚓

Detour *5 mins*
AUGERVILLE-LA-RIVIÈRE

The imposing 14th century château built on the site of a castle has retained its moats, which are fed by the Essonne. It is currently privately owned.

The mairie can be reached by following a continuation of the Promenade des Tours and crossing a road. Continue up the avenue as far as the river where there is a wash-house. Turn left and follow the river as far as a minor road. Turn left and follow the road as far as crossroads, then walk along the path on the right for 200 metres.

3.35Km
0:50

Cross the Essonne at the first crossroads, take a wooded path on the right-hand side that skirts the wall of the château; if the path becomes impassable, continue in the same direction (east) along the edge of the meadow as far as the D948; turn right on to it and follow it for 250 metres.

The GR32 now leaves the department of Seine et Marne and enters Loiret. At the corner of a small wood turn right for 200 metres and then turn left along a hedge. The dirt track leads to the corner of the wall around the grounds of the château on the D831; turn right along it for several metres and then follow a grassy path along the wall behind the cemetery to the edge of Orville.

ORVILLE

Follow the main street through the village. The walk continues straight on along the edge of the hill for 1 kilometre. An uncultivated meadow, on the left before you leave the wood, is authorized for camping. After 200 metres the path begins to climb and leads to a small road on the edge of the hamlet of Buisseau; turn right and follow it down towards the Essonne. At the mill, you can see the well-preserved paddle wheel from the ford. Turn off the road at the left-hand bend and continue straight on between the mill and an outbuilding and then across the footbridge. Turn left and walk along the river and rejoin the D25 near a level crossing. Turn left and follow the road to the church of Briarres-sur-Essonne.

2.5Km
0:35

BRIARRES-SUR-ESSONNE

Church with listed choir and steeple. Mill which was working until 1977; its main wheel and wooden gearing systems have been maintained in perfect condition.

At the church, leave the main street and follow a road that leads diagonally to the left and joins the D27. Turn left and walk 10 metres to the first crossroads.

Detour *1 hr*
PUISEAUX

Small town, which is said to have been first inhabited before the 3rd century. 12th century church of Notre-Dame. Covered market dating from 15th century. Unique 13th century cross in the cemetery. Circuit de la Montagne.

Detour see left. Continue along the D27. A description of this signposted walk can be purchased from the Tourist Information Office in Pithviers.

2.5Km
0:35

The GR32 turns right at the crossroads where there is also a bus stop and 30 metres further on turns left on to a dirt track. After 100 metres it enters a wood to the left; do not turn left, but continue until you reach a field. Follow the hedge on the right-hand side that runs alongside cultivated fields. When you reach a broad path, turn left towards the valley and continue for 150 metres. Then turn left, the signposting is difficult at this point, along the woods at the edge of the fields. The path emerges opposite the fields and lawns of a private estate. A little to the right, the path goes up again to the plateau; when you reach a minor road, turn left and walk along it past the Francorville farm, where there is a dovecote. Cross the Essonne to the mill.

FRANCORVILLE MILL
⌂ ᚼ
Detour 35 mins
Puiseaux

Detour see left. Turn left, walk through the hamlet of Châtillon, across a small road and continue straight on in an east-south-easterly direction along a path that leads to the level crossing on the D26 at the entrance to the village.

Walk to the end of the small poplar-lined road, on the right is a protected area of marshland, then skirt the valley on the right on the hillside for 1 kilometre. Ignore a small road to the left and walk through the straggling hamlet of Foussereau to rejoin the D26 (Ondreville-Puiseaux). Turn right and walk along it for 250 metres. When you arrive opposite the mairie/school, carry straight on for 100 metres and then bear right to reach the Place de l'Eglise in Ondreville-sur-Essonne (right bank). Cross the path that forms part of the walk known as Les hauts de l'Essonne.

Detour 7 mins
VILLEREAU

Cross the bridge over the Essonne. There are two former wash-houses which have been converted into shelters.

6Km
0:85

Walk diagonally across the square and take a street on the left which leads to a grassy square planted with trees. Carry on in the same direction (west). As you follow the footpath, notice the house with walls decorated with bottles which used to be a café. Go as far as a right-hand bend opposite the Groue farm. The Moulin de la Groue is 100 metres on the right. Turn left on to a dirt track, which is soon bordered on the right by a hedge; 600 metres further on it joins a minor road. Turn right on to the road and walk along it for 1 kilometre to a Y-shaped junction. Take

LA NEUVILLE-SUR-ESSONNE
✗ ℽ

*Church of Saint-Amand;
Romanesque porch. There
are inaccessible ruins of a
medieval château in the
middle of the village.*

1.6Km
0:20

Detour *15 mins*
AULNAY-LA-RIVIÈRE
ℽ ▬

*18th-century Château de
Rocheplatte. At the Place de
l'Eglise, turn right on to the
D25 in order to visit the
château.*

Mesnil Farm

4.5Km
1:10

YÈVRE-LE-CHATEL
⚓

*The Rimarde winds round
the village which in the 10th
century was a fortified town.
The 11th and 13th century
church is the Chapelle Saint-
Gault, which was part of an
abbey that stood within the
castle walls. In the cemetery
stands the church of
Saint-Lubin. The site is
dominated by a massive
square keep flanked on each
corner by a circular tower.
The 13th century castle to
which this keep belonged
has disappeared except for
two gate towers and sections
of walls.*

7.5Km
1:45

the left fork, which is a made-up road and,
after 500 metres, turn right into a street which
leads to the Place de l'Eglise in La Neuville-
sur-Essonne.

At the Place de l'Eglise, take the second street
on the right; after 250 metres it joins the
Rimarde at the level of the Guicherie mill
where there is a former wash-house that can
be used as a shelter. Cross the footbridge,
turn left along the fisherman's path and walk
along it for 1.4 kilometres as far as the Mesnil
farm where there is an old mill.

Alternative route to Pithiviers (14.4 kilometres), signposted in yellow. Cross the
Rimarde at the Mesnil farm and walk upstream
on the right bank for 2.75 kilometres and then
on the left bank for 1.75 kilometres. Pass
through Nacelle to Yèvre-le-Chatel.

Leave the village by the road to Estouy. Turn
left on to the first dirt track, skirt the valley of
the Laye de Solvin (the land is private) and
return to the valley of the Oeuf where you will
rejoin the GR32 about 4 kilometres from
Pithiviers opposite the Pont de la Colère.

Mesnil Farm

At Mesnil farm, the GR32 bears slightly to the right away from the Rimarde and towards the Oeuf. During rainy weather, the path can be very soggy. At the stone bridge by the Château de Bouville, which has a fine dovecote and restored mill, turn sharp right on to a forest path and follow it until it begins to climb up the hill.

Alternative route to Pithiviers (14.4 kilometres), signposted in yellow. It goes through the hamlet of Vaux and rejoins the main route at the ruined Petiton mill in the valley of the Rimarde.

2Km
0:30

Before the path starts to climb, turn diagonally to the right on to a small path through a wood that follows the hillside and leads to the Bouffaut mill which is private property. The path runs alongside the mill which is on your left and then crosses the lawn towards the river. Stay on the path close to the water until you reach the undergrowth. Go up into the wood and walk through it for 500 metres until you reach a bend on the small road from Estouy to Yèvre-le-Châtel; turn right and follow the road as far as a crossroads.

Crossroads
Detour 10 mins
ESTOUY
✕ 🍷 🚌
Junction of a small valley with that of the Essonne valley. Short walks (PR routes) are signposted in the Place de l'Église.

Detour see left. Turn right to cross the Essonne, then 200 metres further on turn left at a T-junction and walk up to the village.

Bear left into the Rue du Monceau and take the small road that leads to the Grand Monceau farm; 300 metres further on you will reach a crossroads where there is a view over the valley and the spire of Pithiviers church is visible in the distance. Turn right towards the valley; a short descent leads to a bridge over the Essonne and just before the bridge, turn left on to a path through undergrowth. Skirt some pastures and walk up to the Limosin farm, pass it and take the minor road to the right which crosses an arm of the river. Turn right to the Doureux mill and walk back up the left bank of the Essonne.

2.6Km
0:35

Second crossroads
Detour 15 mins
Estouy

When the road turns 90° to the right, continue straight on along the valley. The GR32 joins a minor road and turns left for 80 metres to the

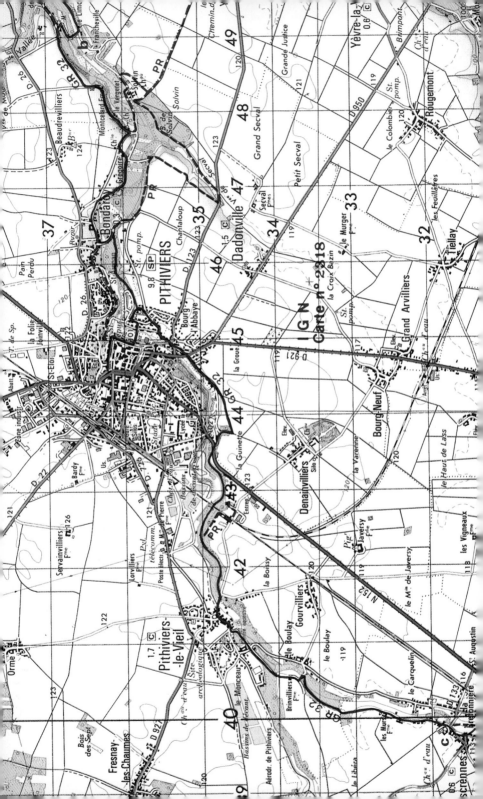

WALK 1

Take the first road on the right running parallel to the valley.

3.5Km
0:45

Detour 5 mins
Grotto of Saint Gregory
Gregory, archbishop of Nicopolis in Armenia, arrived in Pithiviers about the year 1000. He lived near the church of Saint-Martin-le-Seul, at Beaudrevilliers, for the last seven years of his life as a hermit, praying in a grotto. He was buried in the choir of the church of Saint-Martin-le-Seul.

entrance of Montlard farm. Turn right in front of the gate on to a path that winds along the edge of the valley for 750 metres, passes the path leading to the chapel of Notre-Dame des Secours, formerly a place of pilgrimage, and, 50 metres further on, reaches a bend on a minor road.

At this point, a minor road leading off to the left, signposted in yellow, links the GR32 with the alternative route via Yèvre le Chatel. The two routes join at the valley of Solvin.

Detour see left. Take the road to the left for 20 metres, then turn right on to a wooded path running along the bottom of the valley; 100 metres further on the right is the grotto.

Go back up the road on the right for 250 metres, then walk alongside the wall on the left to the church of Saint-Martin-le-Seul, also known as the Chapel of Saint Gregory.

LES MAISONS DE LOIRE
Centres of information on the longest river in France
Orléanais, Touraine, Berry, Perche, Val-de-Loire — merely uttering the name of the provinces that make up the central region of France, the very heart of the country, is to become imbued with a gentle way of life which reflects the exceptional richness of the varying landscapes, from the rustic charms of the Berry to the woodland and pastures of the Touraine. To this gentle way of life the 'Heart of France' has added quality of life, since it is inconceivable that this natural heritage of rivers, woods and forests, which blend so harmoniously to form the natural scenery of our countryside, should not be protected.
  One major achievement provides a perfect illustration of the work of the Regional Council in this area: this is the management, protection and development of the Loire by means of a programme involving not only the strengthening of embankments but also the establishment of the 'Maisons de Loire', centres of information and research on the natural environments of the river that are intended to promote the valleys of the Loire and the priceless asset represented by the variety and elegance of the countryside that lines the river.
MAURICE DOUSSET
President of the Regional Council of Central France
Taken from the magazine 'Espaces pour demain' no. 13, 3rd quarter 1987

Saint-Martin-le-Seul

This is the former parish church of Beaudrevilliers, built in the 10th century. It has a Syrian ground plan: the choir consisted of three naves, each ending in an apse, while benches in the chancel formed galleries on either side of the nave. The churches of Pithiviers-le-Vieil and Yèvre-la-Ville date from the same period and share the same design.

BONDAROY

Y ⚖

The parish church has a tower dating from the 11th and 12th centuries. The fortified manor home of the Taille family is currently being restored. The oldest part is the small round tower, but it also has an imposing street façade dating from the 15th century.

2Km
0:30

At the entrance porch of the church turn left on to a path leading to the wood; after going downhill for 30 metres, you may either continue along the very narrow path or turn right onto a better maintained path that leads, after 50 metres, to the broad path along the bottom of the valley; turn right and follow it for 500 metres until you leave the wood, and then carry on uphill to the road where you have to turn left in order to reach Bondaroy.

After 200 metres, at a crossroads, leave the fortified manor house on your right and continue along the minor road that runs along the valley as far as the first crossroads.

Alternative route to Pithiviers, signposted in yellow, and the GR32. It is a walk of about 30 minutes and leads directly to the bus station in Pithiviers. It rejoins the GR32 at the foot of the ramparts.

Turn left and walk down towards the river Oeuf. Turn left along the river and cross the Pont de la Colère. Opposite the bridge, the GR32 joins the alternative route, signposted in yellow, from Yèvre-le-Chatel.

Immediately after the bridge, turn right on to a grassy track that leads up the right bank of the river. You will see the natural grottoes in the Beauce limestone in the side of the valley. The track comes to the bottom of a slope 500 metres further on. This is being developed as a moto-cross circuit. Walk up this slope, bearing slightly to the left, until you reach the top, near a ruined wall. Go through a wide gap in this wall and go straight on along a wide grassy path bordered on the right by an enclosed wood. A little further on you will come to a pine wood. Skirt the wood and turn right.

About 50 metres beyond the corner of a housing development you will enter Dadonville at the foot of the Chantaloup water tower.

Chantaloup water tower
Detour *20 mins*
PITHIVIERS

Places of interest: the municipal museum; transport museum, with working train; the western promenade at the foot of the city walls built about 1480 by permission of Louis XI; the garden of the town hall near the remains of the 11th century collegiate church of Saint George; the Place du Martroi, with the 15th and 16th century Cathedral of Saint Salomon and Saint Gregory.

Detour see left. Continue straight on along the road bordered by a hedge on the right and 100 metres further on when it joins a road at right angles turn left and walk along for 100 metres. Then turn right into a narrow passageway that goes downhill between two walls. After two bends this reaches the junction of some minor roads, between the houses. Continue straight on, cross the Oeuf and some fields. When you arrive at the bottom of a double flight of stone steps, go up them to the eastern promenade which runs along the foot of the ramparts of the old town. Turn right and follow this for 250 metres to a right-angled bend. In passing, stop to admire the old stone staircase known as the 'postern steps' which leads up along the ramparts to the Place de la Mairie. The alternative route from Bondaroy and Yèvre-le-Chatel joins the GR32 at the corner of the eastern and northern promenades, in the Ruelle du Val Saint-Jean.

Turn left into the northern promenade and cross a road junction on the site of a former town gate; at the end of the avenue turn left onto the western promenade. The Rue de Beauce and then the Rue des Quatre Vents lead to the centre of Pithiviers.

Turn left opposite the water tower and 100 metres further on, turn right down a street. Passing two streets on the right-hand side, the footpath comes to a cross-roads, continue straight on, passing a grocer's shop on the left, until the road forks. Crossing the road on the right you will see the remains of the 11th century priory of Saint Peter, and 250 metres further on you will come to a fork. Take the left-hand road which goes uphill

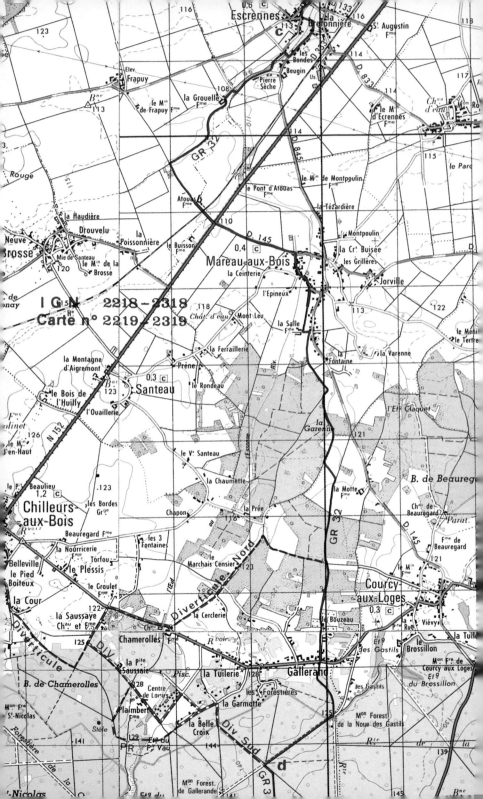

through a wood; after 400 metres you will come to a Y-shaped junction.

Detour *20 mins*
Château de Denainvilliers
The château dates from the 13th century, and a tower of that period still remains. The present château was built in the 17th century.

5.2Km
1:20

Detour see left. Follow the wide and very old path on the left, for 800 metres. It takes you to a minor road which leads to the hamlet of Denainvilliers, opposite the château.

Continue straight on along the dirt track between the fields and meadows, then go down a path on the right at the corner of a wood. After 200 metres, opposite one of the entrances of the Pré aux Sages caravan site, continue straight on to the N152; cross over and follow it to the left for 100 metres along a footpath and then turn right on to a narrow path through a private forest. If you wish to avoid crossing this private forest, it is possible to use the unsignposted alternative route described below.

Alternative route avoiding the private forest. This is subject to change because of the construction of the Pithiviers bypass. Carefully turn left on to the N152 and walk along it for 400 metres, then turn right into a wood and immediately left across farmland. After 500 metres you will come to a small road; turn right and, after the level crossing, right again and then left opposite a house and walk down into the valley where you will rejoin the GR32.

The GR32 goes towards the Oeuf, descending sharply at first and then more gently until it reaches a fisherman's path lined with plane trees. Be careful when you reach the river, because there is a former moto-cross track that is still sometimes used. The route crosses the Pithiviers bypass. Carry straight on for 600 metres until you reach a railway underpass; after this, carry straight on parallel to the river for a further 500 metres. At a T-junction, on a level with Segray and the junction with the alternative route, take the main path on the left. This path is private but authorized for pedestrians.

PITHIVIERS-LE-VIEIL

The church dates from the
10th, 13th and 14th
centuries and was originally
built with a Syrian ground
plan.

3.5Km
0:50

ESCRENNES

The church of Saint-Lubin
dates from the 11th and 14th
centuries. There are the
remains of a 17th century
château, built on the site of a
fortress, and destroyed in
1905.

5.6Km
1:25

When you reach the tarmac road, turn right across the Oeuf and walk up past the village hall to Pithiviers-le-Vieil.

Skirt round the walls of the church on the right-hand side, then turn left and then right. At the end of the road, on a bend, continue straight on down into the valley. The avenue, which is listed, is bordered with plane trees planted in the 18th century and leads to the swimming pool. Carry on in the same direction (south-west) along the side of the pool and then alongside the village pond. At the end of the pond is the Eaux Rouges spring. The short signposted walk 'circuit du Bois de Bellebat' begins at this point. At the crossroads, bear left and walk up, parallel to the valley, to the Brinvilliers farm. Follow the minor road for 50 metres and turn left towards the Oeuf. Before the bridge, turn right on to a dirt track along the river. After 500 metres this leads to a cultivated hollow bordered by a wood. Turn right, then left, and walk parallel to the river to the Murs tree nursery. From here, a minor road leads in the same direction to the Place de l'Eglise in Escrennes.

Walk towards the bridge over the Oeuf and, staying on the same bank, walk up towards the houses. At a fork, within view of the valley bear left; at the next junction turn left on to a path that leads down between vegetable gardens to the river. Cross the footbridge and turn immediately right at the corner of an electricity transformer station; 100 metres further turn right when you come to a small road. After the des Bondes hamlet, go downhill to the right, cross the river and turn left on to a path running parallel to the river which goes to the Grouelle farm. Do not stop in the area around the farm, walk round it on the left-hand side. At this point the GR32 leaves the River Oeuf and follows its tributary the River Laye. Continue straight on (south-west) along the main path which leads across a large area of arable land to a crossroads. Signposting is virtually non-existent for 1.2 kilometres. At the crossroads and a short distance away on the left, you will see a footbridge and, opposite, a small wood. Cross over the footbridge, skirt the little wood and carry on along the dirt track which is very muddy in rainy weather to the Atouas farm. Go over a level crossing and join the N152 at the bus stop for Mareau-aux-Bois. Cross the road and continue along the D145 to a crossroads where there is an electricity transformer station.

Detour 45 mins
BOUZONVILLE-AUX-BOIS
Å ✕ ⚖
At the crossroads continue straight on to the D167.

At the crossroads the GR turns right into Mareau-aux-bois.

MAREAU-AUX-BOIS
✕ ⚖ 🚌
The church of Saint Georges dates from the 11th, 12th and 14th centuries and has an octagonal Romanesque stone spire. The key is at the local policeman's house.

3.4Km
0:50

After the church, continue along the main street of the village, cross the Oeuf and then take the first path to the right, opposite tne grocer's and alongside farm buildings. At the Salle estate where there was once a château, turn left and then, just before the D145, turn right on to a dirt track. At a Y-shaped junction, where signposting in the fields is difficult, ignore the turning on the right and go straight ahead to the edge of the woods. Ignore the pretty private path to the right, and continue straight on along the edge of the woods. Skirt a field on the right-hand side, turn right on to a grassy path and then left on the first path you come to. After 150 metres, you will reach a crossroads.

First crossroads
Detour 10 mins
LA MOTTE FARM
⌂ Å
The farm owes its name to a feudal mound that can still be seen, surrounded by a ditch. Quiet except at weekends. At the crossroads, continue straight on.

1Km
0:15

At the crossroads the GR turns right. Walk through a wood and, 1 kilometre further on, you will come to another crossroads near a plot of cultivated land.

This is the start of a signposted diversion that leads to Chilleurs-aux-Bois.

Second crossroads
Detour 1 hr 15 mins
CHILLEURS-AUX-BOIS
✕ 🍷 ⚖ 🚌

Detour see left. Turn right and 1 kilometre further on, at the corner of a wood, turn left on to a dirt track which can be muddy in wet weather. Walk past the buildings of the Marchais Censier and carry straight on for 1.25 kilometres to the D109 opposite the entrance to the grounds of the Château de

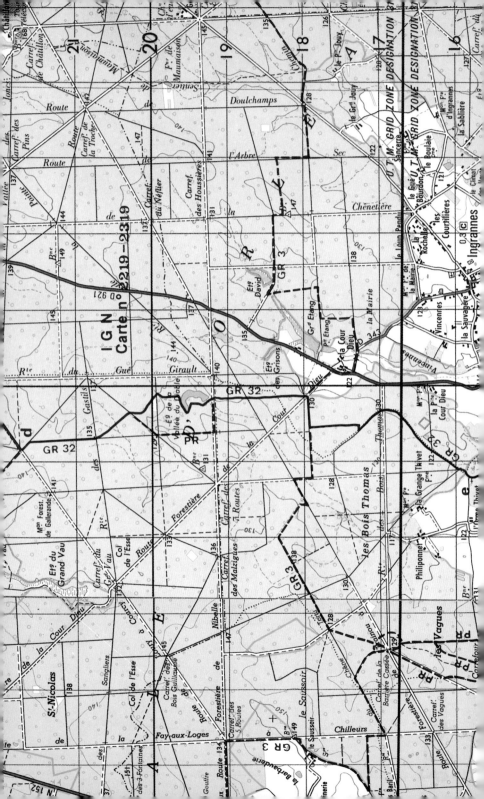

Chamerolles. This is a 16th century château, of square design round a central courtyard which is being restored.

Opposite the entrance turn right on to the D109 and follow it for 1 kilometre to a bend in the road where there is a wayside cross. Turn left here on to the path that skirts the forest and 300 metres further on turn right. On leaving the wood, go on as far as a minor road at La Cour and continue along this road for 500 metres. In the hamlet, turn right and 300 metres further on, turn left into a new housing development. An old path leads off to the right between gardens and comes out at the road that leads left after 400 metres to the central square of Chilleurs-aux-Bois.

Detour *20 mins*
COURCY-AUX-LOGES
✗ ☿

Detour see left. At the second crossroads follow the path on the left to the D145. After the mairie/school, take the path to the left.

First crossroads

From the first crossroads the GR32 continues in the same direction (south) as far as the hamlet of Bouzeau and the D109, which you have to cross. The dirt track turns to the left, becomes a forest track and, 100 metres from an intersection of paths through the Orléans State forest (massif d'Ingrannes), brings you to the home of a warden in the Orléans State forest.

2.25Km
0:35

FORESTER'S LODGE OF THE NOUE DES GÂTIS
Å

Without going up to the forester's lodge, turn right on to the forest path that leads from Loury to Courcy-aux-Loges and walk to a star-shaped intersection known as the 'Carrefour des Fontaines'.

1.1Km
0:15

Carrefour des Fontaines
The numbers of allotments parcels in the forest are indicated by small plaques at intersections and are used as signposts.

This is the starting point for another signposted diversion which will take you back to Chilleurs-aux-Bois.

Detour *1 hr 35 mins*
Chilleurs-aux-Bois

Detour see left. At the intersection, take the second avenue on the right, the Route des Fontaines. At the end of the path and the edge of the state forest, turn right on to the communal forest path and continue along it as far as a small tarmac road. Turn left on to this road and after 250 metres turn right into an avenue that leads, after 300 metres, to a crossroads. Turn left and walk past the chalets in the Domaine de Chamerolles. At the right-hand bend follow the small road for 1.8 kilometres until it bends to the right. Here, you should turn left on to the path running along the edge of the forest. On leaving the wood, go on as far as a minor road at La Cour and continue along this road for 500 metres. In the hamlet, turn right and 300 metres further on, turn left into a new housing development. An old path leads off to the right between gardens and comes out at the road that leads left after 400 metres to the central square of Chilleurs-aux-Bois.

Carrefour des Fontaines

At the intersection the GR32, turns left on to the Carrefour des Fontaines forest road, and 150 metres further on turns right on to the Liteau forest road. At allotments 1150-1152 it bears left along the line that separates them and takes you to a wide grassy avenue, the Route du Chêne au Loup. At this point, depending on whether allotment 1149 is open or closed, walkers will follow one of two routes.

When allotment 1149 is closed, turn right on to the Route du Chêne au Loup and follow it as far as the large intersection of the same name. Take the second avenue on the left which leads south (this is the Route du Liteau). Continue as far as the tarmac Route de Nibelle; turn left on to it and, after 400 metres, you will come to the pond in the Vallée du Diable, where you will turn right to rejoin the GR32. This route is not signposted.

4.1Km
0:1

When allotment 1149 is open, take the following route. Cross the Route du Chêne au Loup and take a track, slightly offset to the right, that leads into allotment 1149. After 150 metres bear left and walk in a straight line through the undergrowth until you reach the Route des Blaireaux. After a slight swing to the right, walk straight on in a southerly direction along the limit of settlement on the edge of the wood.

The huge area on the left is a plantation of young pines

A slight swing to the left will bring you to the pond of the Vallée du Diable opposite a long

and, behind them, a cereal crop.

footbridge. Cross over it, turn left and walk along the pond to the dyke at the end. Walk along the dyke and, at the end, turn right on to the tarmac Route de Nibelle. Cross over and climb on to the embankment and follow the line that separates allotments 988-1026 in a southerly direction. You will cross the forest road from Trainou to Chambon. Continuing to walk south, follow the boundary between allotments 1024 and 1025. At the end of this a wire-netting fence prevents wild boars and badgers from damaging the fields enclosed within the forest; turn left and skirt round it.

Route de la Cour Dieu
Junction with the GR3.
Detour
La Cour Dieu

Detour see left. If you turn left and follow the GR3 for 600 metres (Route de la Cour Dieu), then the D721 to the right you will come to La Cour Dieu.

Detour
INGRANNES
✕

Detour see left. If you turn left and follow the GR3 for 1 kilometre, then follow the D343 for 1.8 kilometres, you will come to the village of Ingrannes.

Cross the Route de La Cour Dieu. For 350 metres, the GR3 and the GR32 share the same path along the Route du Marchais Rond before they branch in separate directions. The GR3 goes off towards the west, while the GR32 goes off left in a southerly direction along the boundary between allotments 1021 and 1022. In sight of a small clump of pines, turn right, then left. The GR continues among coppices and crosses the route du Bois Thomas. After 1 kilometre, you will come to a bend in the Route de La Petite Cour Dieu.

5.3Km
1:20

Detour *10 mins*
FORESTER'S LODGE OF HAUT DES BRUYÈRES
⌂
Turn left and follow the Route de Le Petite Cour Dieu.
This is the limit of the Orléans State forest. The footbridge is situated on the site of an old bridge, now

The GR32 goes down the broad avenue and 450 metres further on, at the end of the avenue, turns left and then right and comes to a makeshift footbridge.

A few metres beyond the footbridge, at the crossroads, continue along the avenue through the forest without changing direction (south-east). Skirt the fence of the Motte estate, then cross the avenue of plane trees

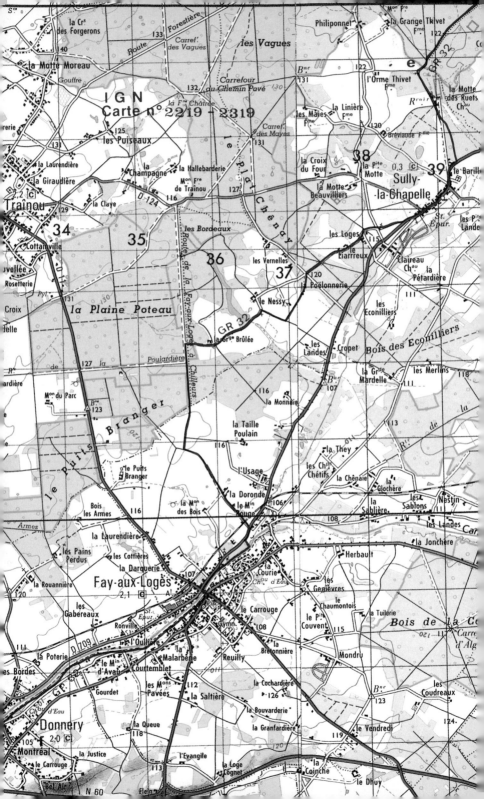

destroyed, which may have been a Roman bridge, since the Roman road between Orléans and Sens followed this route.

SULLY-LA-CHAPELLE
⌂ ▲ ✕ ♟ ♨

The 17th century château de Claireau has two round towers which are the remains of the feudal manor. The château is surrounded by moats fed by the Cens.

8Km
2

FAY-AUX-LOGES
⌂ ▲ ✕ ♟ ♨ ▥

The church of Notre-Dame and Saint-Come has an eight-sided 13th century spire of local stone. There is a former fortified house dating from the 13th century which is currently a

3Km
0:45

that leads up to the château. Take a path that becomes a minor road on a level with some low-roofed houses, parallel to the avenue of plane trees. Turn right on to the D921 and the village of Sully-la-Chapelle.

The GR32 crosses the village and continues for a further 150 metres along the D921. Then, at a slight left-hand bend, it bears right up the embankment and carries on at an angle along a dirt track between cultivated fields, bordered by an electrical power line. When you come to a wayside shrine, turn right on to a small road and then turn immediately left. At an intersection, you will see a wooded avenue opposite you and slightly to the left. Walk along this, passing a house and then a farm on the right that is set back from the path, until you reach a path that is bordered by old trees and may be damp underfoot.

At an intersection of dirt tracks, take the right-hand track and then turn left on to a small road and walk to the isolated farm of La Grange Brûlée, on the edge of the forest. Carry straight on and re-enter the Orléans State forest. Turn left on to the first forest track, the road from Fay-aux-Loges to Chilleurs-aux-Bois, and follow it until you leave the forest. Continue along the dirt track until you come to another path at right angles − (signposting is difficult at this point − turn left on to it and walk through the hamlet of La Doronde and across a level crossing. When you come to the D921, turn right on to it, walk along it for 100 metres and then turn left. The path goes across uncultivated land towards the Orléans canal, which you will join at a disused boat yard. Turn right on to the towpath and walk along it in to Fay-aux-Loges.

Cross the bridge over the canal, then turn right and follow the towpath past the Place de la Mairie; 1.5 kilometres further on, you will come to the junction of the canal and the river Oussance. A wooden footbridge takes the towpath across the river. After a further 1.5 kilometres you will come to an old lock and a bridge over the canal to Donnery.

45

*presbytery and a 16th
century wayside shrine.*

DONNERY

⌂ ✕ ♇ ⚓ 🚌

*The church of Saint-Etienne
dates from the 12th and 13th
centuries. There is a 16th
century stone wayside
shrine on the Mardié road.
The 18th century château de
la Touche has a park and
restaurant.*

Detour *10 mins*

MARDIÉ

🏕 ⚓ 🚌

*The church has a very old
steeple. There is a museum
displaying local arts and
crafts including an old wine
press.*

12.7Km
3:10

Detour *5 mins*

CHÉCY

🏠 🏕 ✕ ♇ ⚓ 🚌

*The Gothic church of Saint-
Pierre has a square
Romanesque belfry. Joan of
Arc came to pray here on 28
April 1429, having crossed
the Loire at Chécy before
entering Orléans. The
Municipal Museum of
Cooperage, Place du Cloître,
has specialized in the history
and production of barrels
throughout the world for the*

The GR32 continues along the towpath and,
150 metres after going under a railway bridge,
reaches the old lock of Pont-aux-Moines. A
pedestrian subway will take you under the
D952 (Orléans-Gien). Take the stone steps on
the left up to ground level and follow the
pavement opposite you. As you cross the
Oussance you will see an old mill. Turn
immediately to the right, at a telephone kiosk,
into the Rue de la Garenne, which is bordered
by gardens. It goes along the sports ground
and then becomes a sandy track. You will
pass, on the left, old paths which lead back to
the centre of the village. Carry on along the
main path to an intersection at the top of the
hill.

Detour see left. Continue along the main path
without going down towards the valley of the
river.

At the crossroads, the GR32 takes the right-
hand path which runs along the crest of the hill
before going down towards the isolated house
known as La Tuilerie. Continue along the little
sandy road (Rue de la Tuilerie) until it ends.
Go down the Rue des Plantes on the right and
you will come out below the village of Chécy,
which overlooks the canal d'Orléans opposite
the Loire.

Detour see left. Cross the bridge over the
canal and walk up the Rue du Port to the Place
Jeanne d'Arc.

Following the GR32, walk as far as the canal,
but do not cross the bridge. On the opposite
bank is a wash-house that can be used as a
shelter. Turn left on to the towpath and 2
kilometres further on, at a bridge, turn left.
After 100 metres turn right on to a wide track
that will take you close to the Loire. Continue
parallel to the river for 150 metres, then cross
a wood and turn right to walk along a stretch of
water, which is the outlet of the canal
d'Orléans into the Loire. At the end of the path,
the GR crosses a humpback footbridge and

transport of all kinds of foodstuffs, both solid and liquid. *Gold coins and jewels from the beginning of the 5th century, discovered in 1952, are displayed in the Bibliothèque Nationale.*

COMBLEUX

🏠 ✕ 🍷 🚃 🚌

Combleux is an old river port which was busy and thriving during the 18th and 19th centuries. Situated at the mouth of the Cense or Oussance, the bed of which was dug out to form the canal d'Orléans (1672 to 1682), the port controlled the traffic between the Loire and the canal. Documents on shipping on the Loire can be seen in the Musée de Châteauneuf-sur-Loire and in the booklets of Mme G. Biton. The port has a 15th century chapel.

SAINT-JEAN-DE-BRAYE

🏠 ✕ 🚃 🚌

The 12th century church was built by Louis VII. Visits can be made to the Bollée bell foundry by appointment. Braye is a Celtic name meaning damp, marshy and fed by streams. It is a name well-suited to the site at a time when the Loire flowed significantly further to the south and formed a damp plain.

2Km
0:30

4.6Km
1:20

turns immediately left on to the Chemin de la Patache which leads back towards the Loire. Follow it as far as an old lock, which is the junction between an arm of the canal d'Orléans and the Loire, and then on to the Île de Combleux, situated between the two arms of the canal.

Opposite the restaurant, the GR32 turns left and goes to a second lock on the second branch of the canal. Cross over the lock and, bearing left, take the small road leading towards the church. Walk round the church, head back towards the canal and turn right on to a broad path closed to motor vehicles; 600 metres further on, cross over a pontoon bridge and enter a wooded area. Almost immediately, walk uphill to the left to a grassy promenade overlooking the Loire and the canal. Follow the path for 1 kilometre, and then at a crossroads, you will come to the ancient market-town of Saint-Jean-de-Braye.

At the crossroads, the GR32 continues along the tarmac road overlooking the canal towpath and passes the edge of various estates. After 1.5 kilometres it goes downhill to the level of a defensive wall and brings you to the Port Saint-Loup crossroads, which is the boundary between Saint-Jean-de-Braye and Orléans. The road on the right, the Rue du Port, leads to the suburb of Bourgogne and the city bus stop line G which is 200 metres away. Continue along the footpath overlooking the Loire to the corner of the Rue Jousselin and the Quai du Roi. The city bus stop line G is 300 metres away.

In order to avoid the traffic, do not walk along the Quai du Roi but bear as far as possible to the left and walk along the edge of the Loire. Go under the Paris-Vierzon railway line and then under the new road bridge over the Loire. At this point you will find yourself in front of the Motte Sanguin Centre which is also a gîte. A little further on, along the slight incline that was the site of the first settlements in Orléans, you will come to the quays along the Loire. Here you may join an unsignposted alternative route of 1.2 kilometres which will take you through the old quarters away from the bustle of the modern city to the Pont Georges V.

Alternative route to the Pont George V. Turn left into the Rue neuve de Saint-Aignan and walk as far as the church of the same name; turn left into the Rue Coligny and walk parallel to the Loire as far as the Rue Royale which joins the Pont Royal on the left and passes arcaded houses. This route will give you a glimpse of the Gallo-Roman and medieval site of the city. The remains of the city wall date from the 3rd, 4th, 13th and 14th centuries.

If you follow the GR32, it will take you along the quays to the Pont Georges V.

Pont Georges V, Orléans

*Magnificent stone bridge
over the Loire,
formerly known as
the Pont Royal, built
in the 18th century and
inaugurated by the Marquise
de Pompadour.*

At this point GR32 ends, and joins the GR3 which goes from Orléans to Saumur.

Pont Georges V, Orléans

WALK 2

ORLÉANS

🏠 ⌂ ⛺ ✕ ⚑ ⛲
🚌 🚂 ℹ

Situated on the north bank of the Loire at the most northerly point of the river's course and devastatingly bombed during 1940. An important centre of communication between the Loire and Paris throughout the ages, Joan of Arc, heroine of Orléans, entered the besieged city on 29 April, 1429, and ejected the English from their last bastion, the Fort des Tourelles, within eight days. This feat, which certainly influenced the outcome of the Hundred Years' War, is still celebrated annually. Gothic Cathedral, St-Croix. Choir begun by Henri IV. Glass in aisle windows (1893) depicts scenes from life of Joan of Arc. Old churches and buildings from 16th, 17th and 18th centuries; architectural rarities can be seen in almost every street.

5Km
1:15

The walk starts at the Vieux Pont in Orléans, on the right bank of the Loire, at the end of the Rue Royale. The GR3 goes in a westerly direction (towards Blois) along the promenade bordering the river. After a road bridge, it divides into two avenues; follow the one closest to the Loire. The GR passes close to a factory and then continues along a road which becomes a path to the camp site of Saint-Jean-de-la-Ruelle (see map ref B). It continues straight on, goes under a motorway bridge, and passes an island that is a designated bird-watching centre (migratory birds) of the University of Orléans. The path widens into an avenue and leads to the church of La Chapelle-Saint-Mesmin.

LA-CHAPELLE-SAINT-MESMIN

🏠 ⛺ ✕ ⛲ 🚌 🚂

*(see map ref C)
11th century church;
7th century grotto of
Saint-Mesmin.*

5Km
1:15

At the church of la Chapelle-Saint-Mesmin, the GR continues straight on along a road as far as the camp site. At this point, it leaves the road and continues in the same direction along a dirt track through a wood. Some distance further on, turn on to the right-hand path and climb up to the embankment along the Loire.

The GR turns left (south-west) to follow this embankment; the signposting is widely spaced. You will pass an isolated house and go under high-voltage electricity cables before

coming to the Bouverie farm. After some more high-voltage cables, the GR comes to the funfair at Fourneaux beach.

Plage de Fourneaux
Detour *15 min*
FOURNEAUX
3Km 🏠 ✕ 🍷 🍺 ▦
0:45 *Hamlet in the commune of Saint-Ay.*
Follow the road in a northerly direction to join the N152.

From Fourneaux beach the GR follows the road in a southerly direction and continues along a path on the edge of the Loire. It crosses a stream and then, climbing slightly, goes through Le Coteau and L'Evêché to arrive close to the beach of Saint-Ay. Walk along the boundary wall of an estate and you will come to Saint-Ay.

Shipping on the Loire

Commercial shipping on the Loire flourished until the middle of the 19th century: ships sailing down the Loire exported silks produced in the workshops of Tours, while, in the opposite direction, the region imported, via Nantes, salt from the Guérande peninsula, products of Louisiana, and vines from Bordeaux.

Along the river and its tributaries are the remains of former ports, including those at Chouzé, which has retained its moorings, Chinon and Saint-Avertin (the latter located on the canalized section of the Cher). Sailing downstream with the current, the long, flat boats with their rectangular sails took advantage of westerly winds on the return journey.

The corporation of 'merchants', founded in the 14th century had its head-quarters in Orléans, but Amboise and Tours were also important staging posts. The ships were mainly used for transporting merchandise, but many of them also carried passengers. The journey downstream between Orléans and Nantes took six days, while the return journey, with favourable winds, took between 15 and 20 days.

Apart from timber rafts, there was a great variety of types of ship, all of them flat-bottomed. Until the beginning of this century, long after the demise of passenger-carrying ships on the Loire, flat-bottomed barges were used to transport grain and cattle. At the end of the journey downstream, the deal tubs were destroyed, and the wood was salvaged at Nantes. Lighters, with their square sails that could be raised to a height of 20 metres and enormous rudders, were by far the most important boats on the Loire. They usually sailed in convoys, towed by the 'mother vessel' and preceded by a sounding vessel which measured the depth of the water and gave warning of sandbanks.

From 1832 onwards, sail power gave way to steam: the journey from Tours to Nantes now took only two days, but there were frequent accidents caused by exploding boilers. Paddle boats, said to be incapable of exploding, then began to ply the river. In 1843, no fewer than 100,000 passengers travelled between Moulins and Brittany. However, the arrival of the railways, with the major marshalling yard at Saint-Pierre-des-Corps and, above all, the opening of the line from Paris to Saint-Nazaire, heralded the end of river traffic.

BERNARD HENNEQUIN

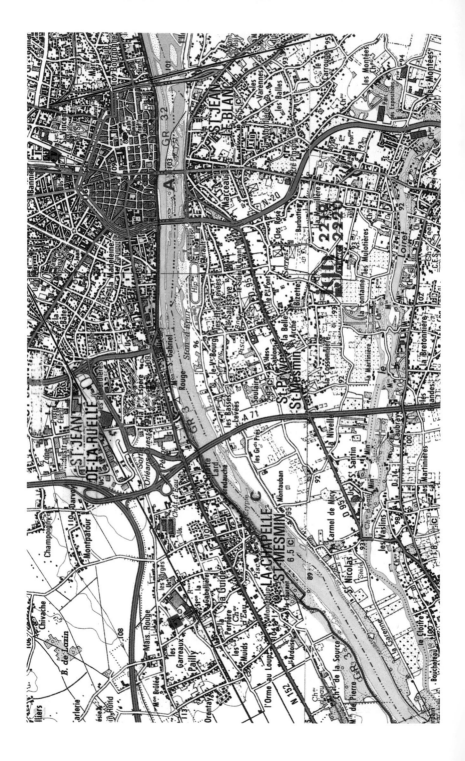

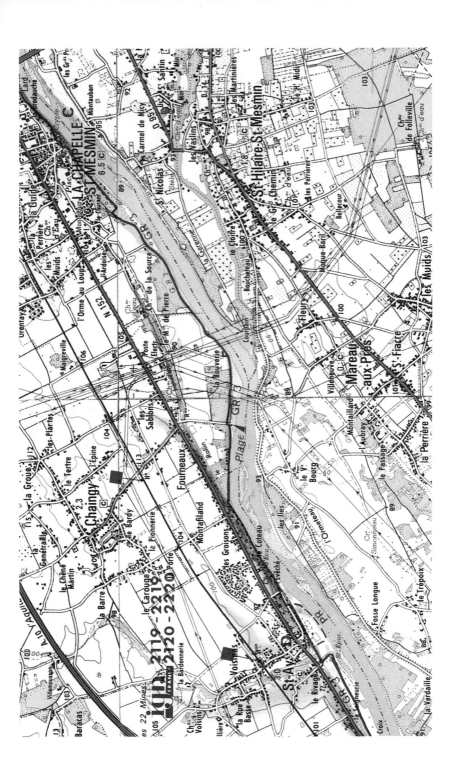

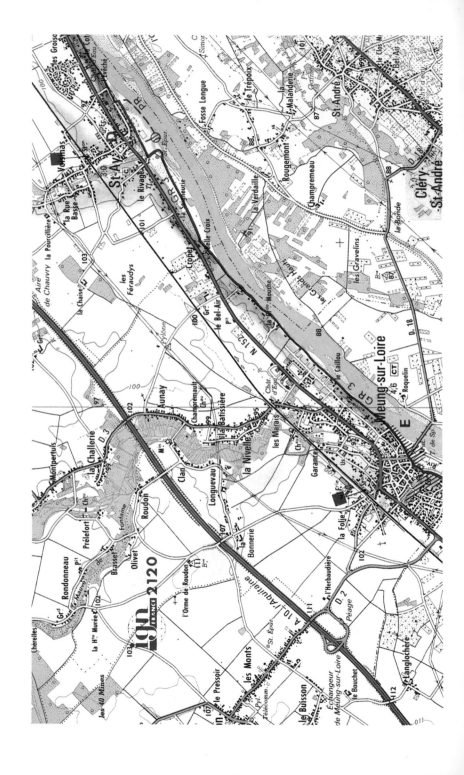

SAINT-AY

🏠 🛏 ✕ ⚓ ♀ 🚌 🚃

(see map ref D)
The port of Saint-Ay, like all
the ports in towns and
villages along the Loire,
must have been active from
the pre-Roman era until the
development of the railways.
The unique Loire shipping
fleet included sailing boats

6Km *that transported goods and*
1:30 *horse-drawn barges that*
carried passengers. The
salmon and shad fisherman
used flat-bottomed barges
(some still exist today). The
mills on the water were
moored to the banks and
floated on the river.
There is a museum of
shipping on the Loire at
Châteauneuf-sur-Loire.

MEUNG-SUR-LOIRE

🏠 🛏 ✕ ♀ ⚓ 🚌

🚃

(see map ref E)
12th and 13th century
church, with an 11th century
spire, dedicated to Saint
Liphard, built on the site
where this monk founded a
monastery in the 6th
century. The 13th century
château adjoining the
church, residence of the
bishops of Orléans. Famous
local wines are Gris Meunier
and Auvernat.

8Km
2   **Caution:** *the non-tarmac*
section of the path between
Meung and Beaugency,
situated in the commune of
Baule, is closed between
7 p.m. and 5 a.m.

In Saint-Ay, the GR3 follows the Rue de la Galère and joins the Chemin de la Hausseraie (the former towpath before the silting up of the Loire); it crosses the François Rabelais alley and carries straight on to a small road; walk along this road in a southerly direction towards the camp site. Then go down a path that passes in front of the water-purification station and walk along between the Loire and the estates bordering it. You will pass Belle-Croix, Grande-Mouche and Caillou. The GR follows a tree-lined avenue (camping in summer) which leads to the Meung-sur-Loire suspension bridge.

The GR3 does not cross the bridge but continues straight on, crosses the Mauve and follows the road that runs alongside it. It follows the *promenade des Mauves* and then continues straight on (south-east) along the river on the southern bank to the junction with the Loire.

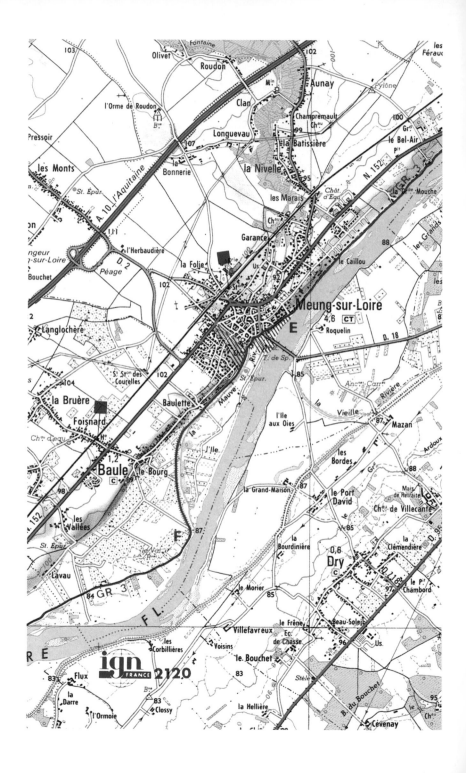

Detour *15 mins*
BAULE
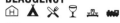
(see map ref F)
*Take the road on the right
into the village.*

BEAUGENCY

(see map ref G)
*15th century timber house in
the Place du Martroi; the
11th century church of Saint-
Etienne; the clock tower
(former gate of Vendôme);
the Renaissance town hall;
the Maison des Templiers;
the tower of Saint-Firmin;
the church of Notre-Dame
(former 12th century abbey
church restored in the 17th
century); Caesar's tower (an
11th century keep); Château
Dunois (15th century), which
houses a regional museum;
Devil's Tower, the remains
of an abbey founded in 1580
by Simon I; the bridge over
the Loire with six central
gothic arches that date from
the 16th century; the 12th
century porte de Tavers.*

8Km
1:45

Detour *45 mins*
VERNON
*Walk to the SNCF station at
Beaugency (north-west) and
then through Baltan and Le
Verger.*

LESTIOU
(see map ref H)
*Curious open wash house;
salt warehouse – an old
building on the river Lien. On
the left bank of the Loire is
the nuclear power station.*

2Km
0:30

The GR continues along the path that runs alongside the river close to the embankment, passes through orchards, crosses a road (spot height 84) and carries on along the Loire as far as the promenade in Beaugency.

From the promenade at Beaugency, the GR3 continues along the quay by the Loire. At Barchelin, follow the path towards the water-purification station; walk round it and follow a path across fields and meadows to a cross-roads (spot height 83).

At the crossroads, turn left and rejoin the path along the Loire. The GR turns away from the Loire, crosses a small river called the Lien and leads to the edge of Lestiou.

From Lestiou, turn left (south-west) towards le Tertre. At the entrance to the hamlet, turn off the road and continue on the embankment along the Loire until it joins the D70 road.

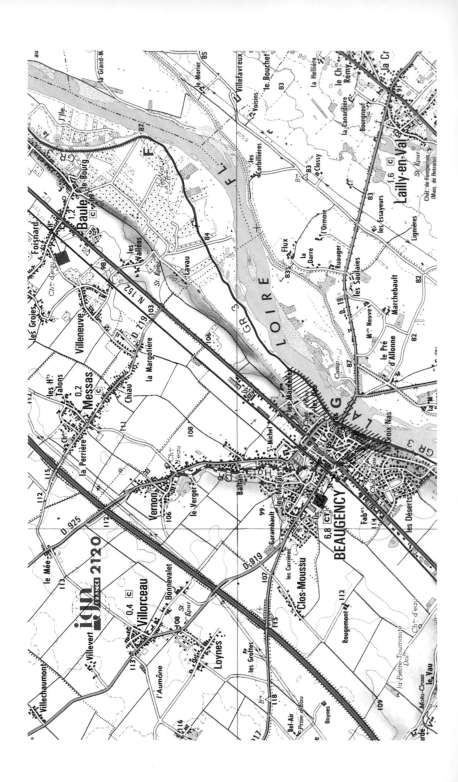

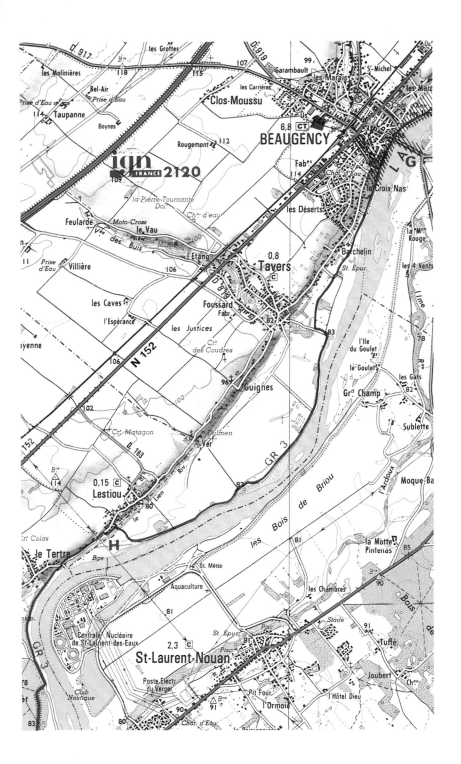

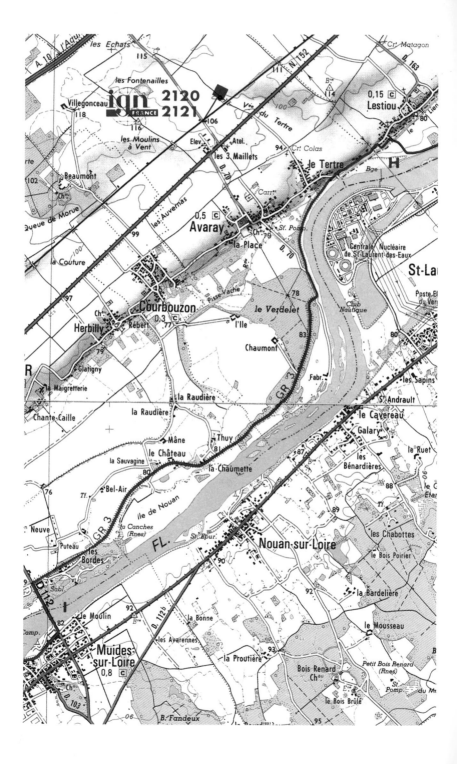

D70
Detour *15 mins*
AVARAY
Ⴤ ☂ ⛟ ▭
13th century château
surrounded by moats.
Follow the road from Le
Tertre or the D70 (north-
west).

6Km
1:30

Follow the D70 in a southerly direction; 300 metres further on the road enters the Verdelet wood and then comes to the embankment, which it follows. You will pass the farm at La Chaumette, go through Le Château, skirt round the Île de Nouan and, after the hamlet of Les Bordes, you will come to the D112.

D112
Detour *1 hr*
MER
⌂ ✗ Ⴤ ☂ ⛟ ▭
Follow the D112 in a north-
westerly direction.

1Km
0:15

The GR3 turns on to the bridge over the Loire and enters Muides-sur-Loire.

MUIDES-SUR-LOIRE
⌂ ⚓ ✗ Ⴤ ☂ ▭
(see map ref I)

4Km
1

In Muides-sur-Loire, turn right (south-west) onto the road that runs alongside the camp site. Continue straight on along the grassy embankment overlooking the Loire as far as the Bel Air district at the entrance of Saint-Dyé-sur-Loire.

Château de Chambord

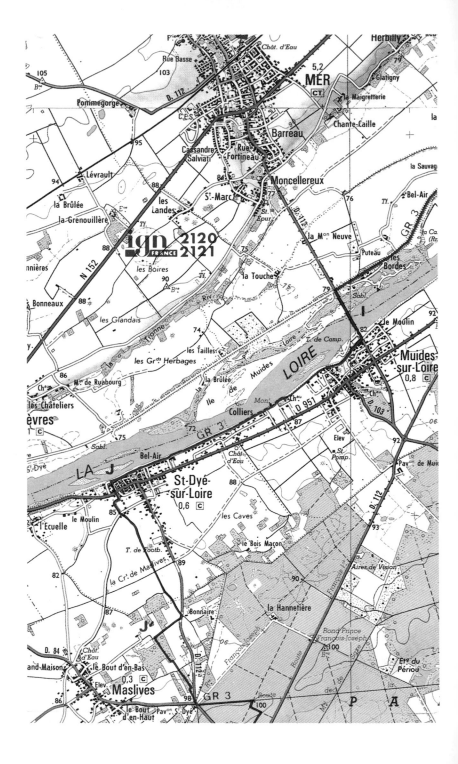

SAINT-DYÉ-SUR-LOIRE

🏠 Å ✕ ⟨ ⚓ 🚌

The village owes its name to the hermit saint Deodatus (meaning god-given; the French 'Dieu-donne' hs become shorted to Dié). Born in Bourges in the 5th century, Deodatus lived at Chabris-sur-Cher and then at Saint-Dié. The village was a stopping place on the pilgrimage route to Santiago de Compostela in Spain. 16th century church built on the site of an earlier church built over the grotto of Deodatus; the sarcophagus of the saint can be seen in the choir.

3Km
0:45

Crossroads
(see map ref J')
Detour *15 mins*
MASLIVES
🏠 ✕ ⟨ ⚓
Continue along the main path (south-west) to le Bout-d'en-Bas.

4Km
1

Detour *45 mins*
MONTLIVAUT
🏠 Å ⚓
From Maslives follow the D84 (north-west) as far as the village.

CHAMBORD
🏠 ✕ ⟨ 🚌
Visit the 16th century château, the park and the village.

3.5Km
1

From Bel-Air, continue along the Loire. A little before the end of the quay (see map ref J), turn left into the Rue de la Renardière, cross the D951 and follow the Rue de Maslives (south-east). Go round three bends and continue straight on along a dirt track across fields. Join the D112a before Bonnaire, but turn off this road very soon at a fork, taking the right-hand path in the direction of a small wood. It will take you to a crossroads.

At the crossroads the GR3 bears to the left (south-east) and leads to the crossroads of the Pavillon-Saint-Dyé, which marks the entrance to the park of Chambord. Walk through the gate and along the avenue known as the Route de la Reine (east) for 600 metres; bear right and continue along a winding path as far as the D112a. Follow the road in the south-easterly direction as far as Rond François 1er crossroads (see map ref K). From here, bear right (south-west, then south) onto a road that leads to the edge of the car park at the Château of Chambord.

The GR3 now follows the same route as the GR3C as far as the hamlet of Rue-de-Meneuil. The footpath turns left off the road to the château and continue in a westerly direction along D33, known as *Route Charles X*; 250 metres further on it turns right and then follows a path along the Cosson. You will rejoin the D33; turn right and follow it as far as a crossroads at the entrance to La-Chausée-le-Comte.

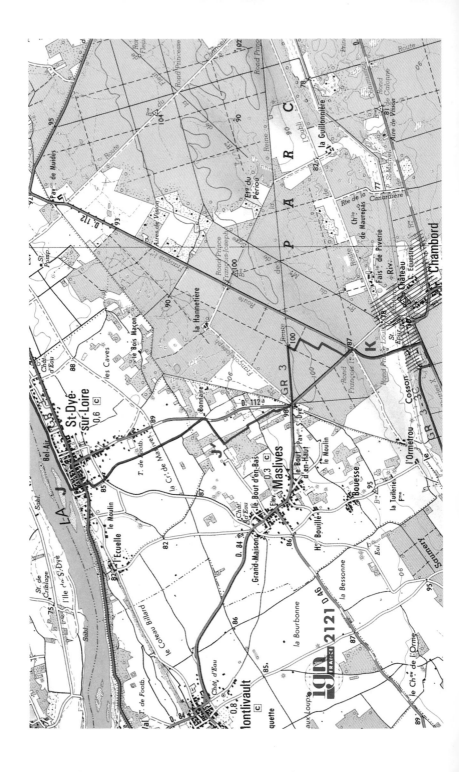

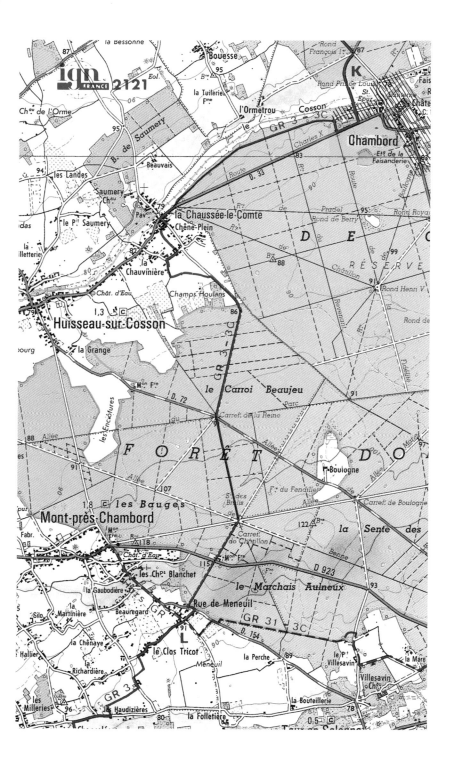

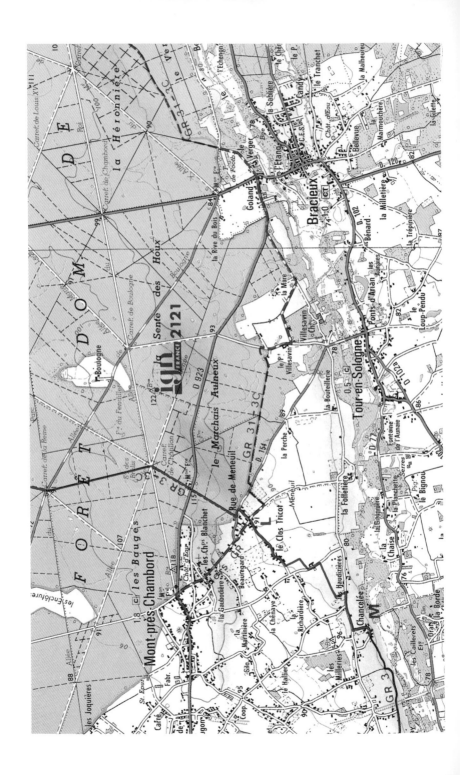

The mirage of Chambord

Everybody is astonished by Chambord. You come here, aware of its reputation and determined to avoid clichés. You cross the 24-kilometre wall that separates the park from the Sologne and, in the central avenue, you see the extraordinary turrets loom into view. The first time I saw Chambord, it was snowing. A layer of cotton wood muffled all sounds and intensified the melancholy of the place until it became almost unbearable, but the air remained limpid. It seemed to me that I was looking at the prettiest of all villages, astonishingly suspended in the sky. It was the mirage of Chambord, as it had been described in the last century in the 'Magasin Pittoresque'. I have seen it often since then, in other seasons, but I have retained a certain fondness for Chambord in winter.

Nor surprisingly, Chambord has been an inspiration to writers. Chateaubriand said of it: 'From afar, the building is an arabesque. It resembles a woman whose hair has been tousled by the wind'.

Vigny, a proud inhabitant of nearby Loches, also expressed his pleasure. 'Four leagues from Blois, one hour away from the Loire, in a small, low-lying valley, between swampy bogs and a wood of large oaks, far away from all roads, the traveller suddenly encounters a royal, or rather a magical château. It is as if a genie from the Orient, propelled from some magic lamp, had carried it off during one of the thousand and one nights, snatching it from the land of the sun to hide it in the country of cloud and mist'.

ARMAND LANOUX

LA-CHAUSÉE-LE-COMTE
🏠 ✕ ♀ ▭

Hamlet in the commune of Huisseau-sur-Cosson.

Detour *30 mins*
HUISSEAU-SUR-COSSON
🏠 ✕ ▭ ▭

7Km
1:45

From the crossroads at La Chaussée-le-Comte, continue along the D33 (south-west).

Turn off the D33 at La Chaussée-le-Comte and follow the road to the left towards Chêne. After 100 metres, continue along the Rue de la Tuilerie and then turn right towards La Chauvinière; walk across some fields and join a road that enters the national forest of Boulogne. Follow it as far as La Reine crossroads; there, take the first path on the left (south-east) and follow it as far as the Châtillon crossroads. Here, take the third tarmac path to the right (south-west); cross the D923 near to an old forester's lodge. The GR continues straight on to the edge of the forest. When you come to the D154, turn left (east); 100 metres further on, turn right and walk to a crossroads (spot height 91) in the hamlet of Rue-de-Meneuil.

RUE-DE-MENEUIL
▭

*(see map ref L)
Starting point of the GR31, which, together with the GR3C, turns left (south-east) towards Bracieux.*

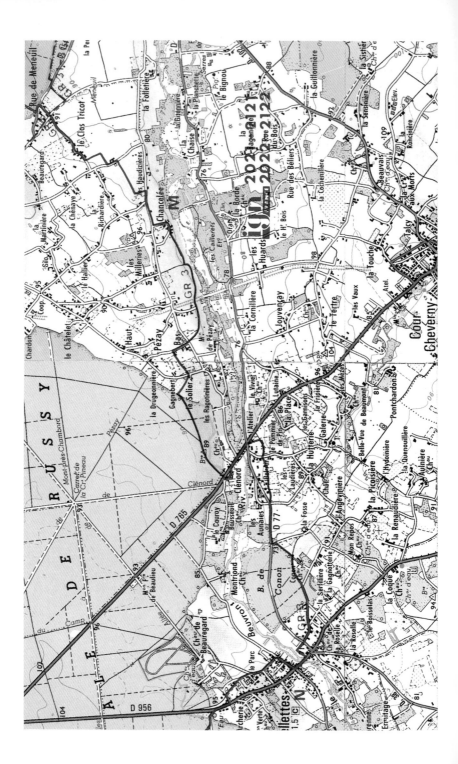

Detour *20 mins*
MONT-PRÈS-CHAMBORD
🏠 ✗ ⏱ 🚃

2Km
0:30

From the junction, take the road on the right (north-west) and then follow the D154 as far as the junction with the D923, where you turn left.

Chancelée
(see map ref M)

4Km
1

CLÉNORD
🚃

1Km
0:15

L'Atelier
Detour *45 mins*
COUR-CHEVERNY
🏠 ▲ ✗ ⏱ 🚃

17th century château, 1 kilometre south of Cour-Cheverny.

3Km
0:45

From L'Atelier, follow the N765 in the direction of Romorantin (south-east).

CELLETTES
🏠 ▲ ✗ ⏱ 🚃

(see map ref N)
Wines can be bought from growers (Sauvignon, Gamay, Pinot, VDQS, Cheverny).

4Km
1

Detour *15 mins*
Château de Beauregard
This 16th century, Renaissance-style château is

From the crossroads (spot height 91) marking the junction with the GR31 and GR3C, the GR3 continues straight on (south-west) and passes through Le Clos Tricot. At the far end of the hamlet, turn left on to a path that will take you across fields and meadows. Pass close to Les Haudizières, follow a small road in a westerly direction for 500 metres and then turn left (south) into the first road that will bring you to Chancelée.

As you leave the hamlet of Chancelée, turn off the road and follow the Beuvron in a south-westerly direction for 1.5 kilometres. Cross the road to Clénord. Continue straight on along the houses of Pézay-Bas, turn left and walk to Le Solier; cross the road. Shortly afterwards, you will enter the Russy national forest. After crossing the D765 you will come to Clénord.

The GR leads in a westerly direction round the hamlet of Clénord and rejoins the D765, which it follows as far as a crossroads at L'Atelier.

At the Atelier crossroads, turn right (south) on to a path which goes uphill to begin with and follow it to the first crossroads. Turn right, cross a minor road at Bel-Air and continue straight on in a westerly direction joining the D77. At the entrance to the Bois de Conon (spot height 73) bear left towards the Château de Conon. Skirt round the outer wall of château to the right on the Chemin de Charlemagne until you reach a small road leading to Cellettes. At the junction with the D77, carry straight on and turn right round the camp site. Follow the River Beuvron to the left. At the bridge, cross over and enter Cellettes.

At Cellettes, take the first street on the right after the bridge; follow it as far as the church, then turn left (north-west) and continue straight on as far as the cemetery.

Shortly after the cemetery, at a fork, the GR goes along the left-hand path and then joins D956 for 250 metres (north). Turn left at the water tower and then enter the Russy national forest along the Allée Verte; after 100 metres, follow the Allée du Coteau (north-west). Cross

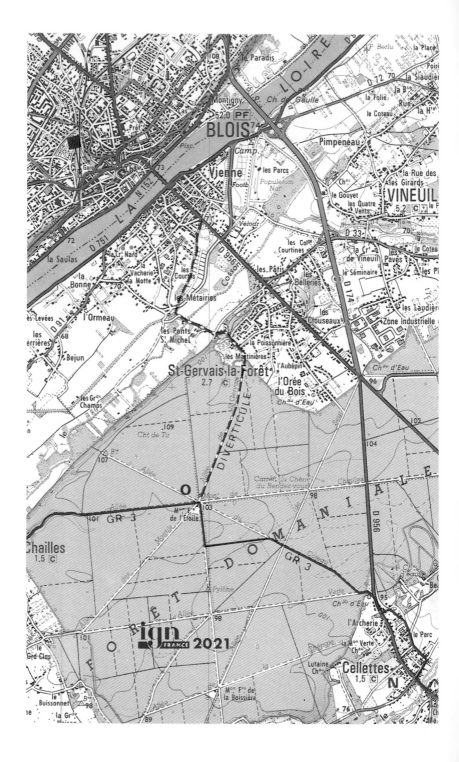

said to be a former hunting lodge built during the reigns of François 1er and Henri II. At the crossroads, before the cemetery, follow the road in a north-easterly direction.

Crossroads
Detour *1 hr 30 mins*
Blois

SAINT-GERVAIS-LA-FORÊT
⚠ ✗ ☕ 🚉 🚌

the Allée de Seur and, 100 metres further on, turn left (west) on to a forest track. When forestry work is going on, continue along the Allée du Coteau as far as the Etoile crossroads. The GR3 carries on along this track in a westerly direction, then turns right (north) on to a tarmac path leading to the Etoile crossroads.

Detour see left. From the crossroads opposite the forester's lodge, follow the Allée de Saint-Gervais as far as Les Martinières, a hamlet in Saint-Gervais-la-Forêt.

The detour continues north-west along the road. Cross the Cosson at Les Ponts Saint-Michel; when the road bends, carry straight on

Château de Blois

73

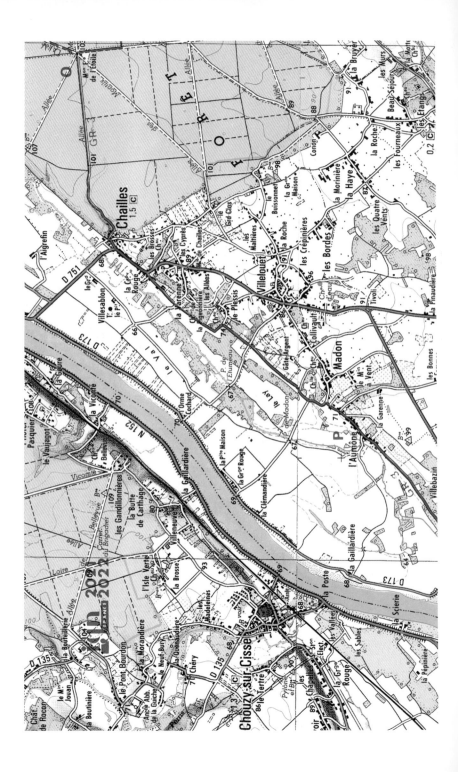

Le Château de Blois

For Françoise, whom he loved and whose 'wiles' he cherished, the king saw to it that festivities became more and more frequent; in so doing, he recreated on the banks of the Loire the atmosphere of his beloved duchy of Milan. But he had great affection for Queen Claude, and for her he ordered the work of Louis XII at Blois to be continued. The wing that now bears the name of King François 1er was to have been named after the queen.

This building with the double façade – the one with the loggias overlooking the town and the other, in the courtyard, framing the famous staircase – this structure that is so typically French, despite its Florentine pilasters, with its lissome design, its foliated scrolls, its basket capitals and those ribbons that mingle with all the motifs, was indeed a suitable residence for that gentle and melancholy sovereign, the retiring, pale Queen Claude, a humble flower beside the royal oak. On the octagonal, openwork staircase – 'sculpted like a Chinese ivory', said Balzac — beside the flamboyant salamander can be seen the queen's ermine, as white as her soul. The moon, her emblem, can also be seen, accompanied by the queen's motto: Candida candidis, which, freely translated means: 'I offer my heart to great-hearted people'.

Here, the Renaissance ceases to be an ornament and becomes an architectural style. Much later, La Fontaine, contemplating the François 1er wing of the Château of Blois, was to say: 'I think it would be difficult to find a more pleasant and agreeable aspect. There are numerous small galleries, small windows, small balconies and small ornaments, arranged without regularity and without order. The whole adds up to something great which is most delightful'. La Fontaine was a perceptive man! In the 17th century, the Renaissance was hated!

ANDRÉ CASTELOT

BLOIS

🏠 🏠 ⛺ 🍴 🍷 ⚓

🚌 🅸

13th century château (son et lumière); Cathedral of Saint-Louis; church of Saint-Vincent-de-Paul; church of Saint-Nicholas; Hôtel d'Alluye (pavillon d'Anne de Bretagne).

2.5Km
0:40

CHAILLES

🏠 ⛺ 🍴 ⚓ 🚌

along a path bearing north-east. Cross a road at Les Métairies. Climb on to the embankment, pass through Les Courtils and turn left (north-west) on to the D956. Go along the road as far as the bridge over the Loire. Cross the river and walk into the centre of Blois.

From the Etoile crossroads the GR3 follows the Allée de Chailles (west) and after a winding section towards the end reaches a crossroads in Chailles.

From the Chailles crossroads continue in a south-westerly direction through the village

75

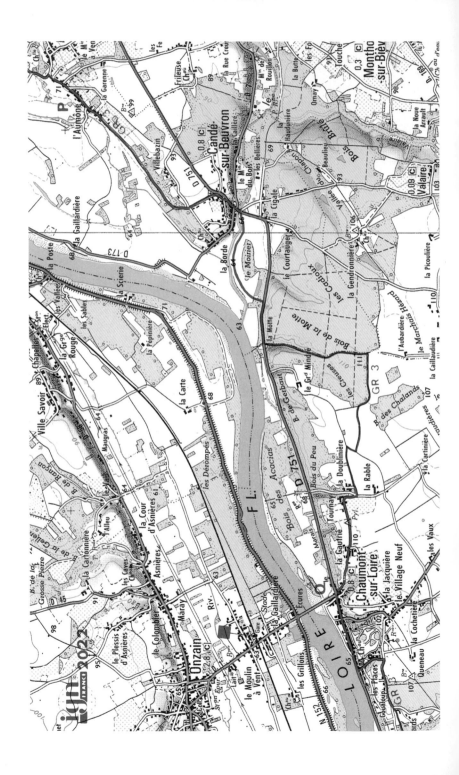

until you join the D751; follow it as far as la Croix Rouge, and there carry straight on (south-west) on the road that runs parallel to the stream known as Le Lay. Cross the road to Varenne. At a junction on a bend, ignore the road to the Château de Plessis on your left. Cross the road to Villelouet and continue through the vineyards of Gâte-Argent. Ignore the roads to the Château de Madon on your left and continue to L'Aumône (see map ref P). Carry straight on as far as the D751 and walk into Candé-sur-Beuvron.

7Km
1:45

CANDÉ-SUR-BEUVRON
🏠 ⌂ Å ✕ 🚃 🚌

The GR3 continues through Candé-sur-Beuvron along the D751, crosses the Beuvron and then follows it downstream and rejoins the D751.

Caution when the river is in spate, stay on the D751 for the first part of the walk.

7Km
1:45

Turn right and west and follow the road as far as La Motte. Turn left here (south), cross La Motte wood, turn right (spot height 111) and skirt the edge of Creuses wood. At a junction, follow the path (west) that leads to the hamlet of La Doublinière. Then follow a small road through Tournay and La Gautrié. Carry straight on along a path that goes down towards the Loire. The GR rejoins the D751 and enters Chaumont-sur-Loire.

CHAUMONT-SUR-LOIRE
🏠 Å ✕ 🚃 🚌 🛈
(see map ref Q)
Fortified chateau with large crenelated towers with panoramic view over the Loire.

6Km
1:30

Detour *15 mins*
ONZAIN
🚃
Cross the river and continue straight on along the D1 as far as the railway station.

At Chaumont-sur-Loire, the GR3 leaves the bridge to the right and continues west along D751 for 1 kilometre. It then bears left towards Les Places. At the second junction, it turns right (west), passes through Goualoup and follows a path leading down towards the D751. Shortly before this road, turn on to a by-road that you will leave 500 metres further on at a bend to follow a path leading to Le Meunet. Continue west along a road that passes through the hamlets of Le Rosne and Les Beaudries and enters the village of Rilly-sur-Loire.

RILLY-SUR-LOIRE
🏠 ✕ 🚃 🚌
(see map ref R)

After the church of Rilly-sur-Loire, turn left along the D28a (south) between the houses for 300 metres and follow a path (south-west)

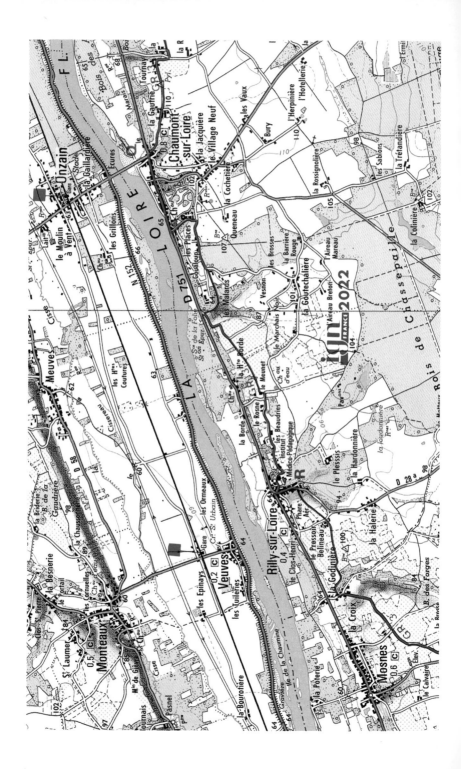

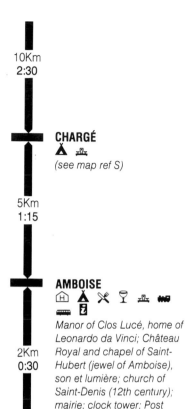

10Km
2:30

CHARGÉ
(see map ref S)

5Km
1:15

AMBOISE

Manor of Clos Lucé, home of Leonardo da Vinci; Château Royal and chapel of Saint-Hubert (jewel of Amboise), son et lumière; church of Saint-Denis (12th century); mairie; clock tower; Post museum.

2Km
0:30

towards the hamlets of Le Pressoir-Bellineau and La Godinière. Continue along a small road (south-west) as far as the hamlet of Les Hauts-Noyers and cross the Mosnes road. The GR3 passes La Maillardière, to the south of Le Grand-Village, and L'Ours farm. Walk through the hamlets of Vau and d'Artigny and into the village of Chargé.

The GR continues through Chargé towards Le Bourg-Neuf and turns right after the château. At L'Arsandrie, bear right at the first cross-roads, then before the Château de La Briquet-erie turn left on to the road through the vineyards. Cross the D31b and carry straight on at the Chaumières crossroads as far as the Bel-Air water tower; here, follow the road that leads west through La Motte to the foot of the Château d'Amboise.

The GR3 does not cross the bridge at Amboise but joins the D61 as far as the edge of Le Pied-Courtaud. Turn right, cross the D81 and enter the district of Maletrenne. The footpath bears right and continues as far as the junction with the D31.

Le Clos-Lucé and Leonardo da Vinci

Le Clos-Lucé, close to Amboise, is a Renaissance manor house, spoilt by history. Leonardo da Vinci worked there for three years and died there in 1519, in the arms of François I, so it is said. In the light of the king's timetable at this period, this is impossible. Fifty models of machines, made from his sketches, can be seen at Le Clos-Lucé, but the house was also the residence of noble ladies. Charles VIII had a delightful chapel built there for his pious wife, Anne of Brittany. She liked to come here to ask for Divine assistance, her Book of Hours in her hands, while her son, Charles-Orland, played in the gardens. Marguerite de Navarre, author of the Heptameron, held a literary court at Le Clos-Lucé towards which François I, a great patron of letters and the arts, was to acknowledge his debt. Finally, the wife of Giocondi, 'La Gioconda', or Mona Lisa, sat enthroned in the studio at Le Clos-Lucé: Leonardo da Vinci had brought his wonderful masterpiece from Italy because he could not bear to be separated from it.

PHILIPPE LEVÉE

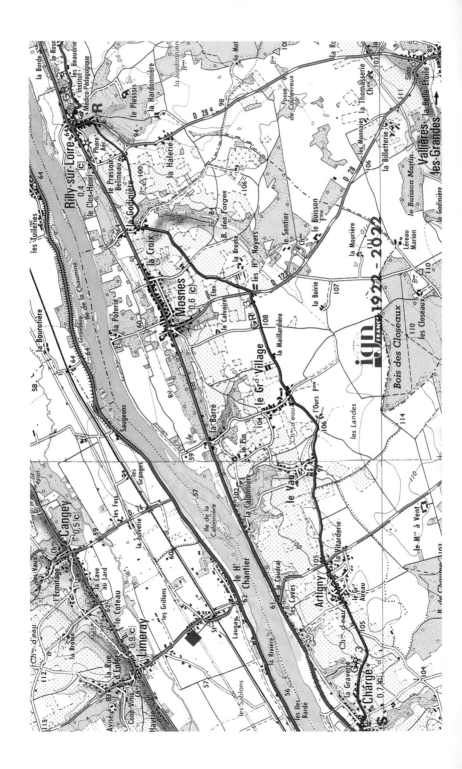

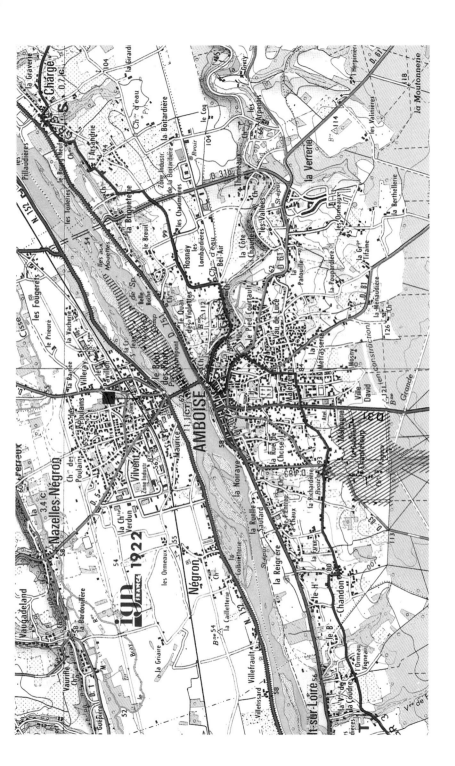

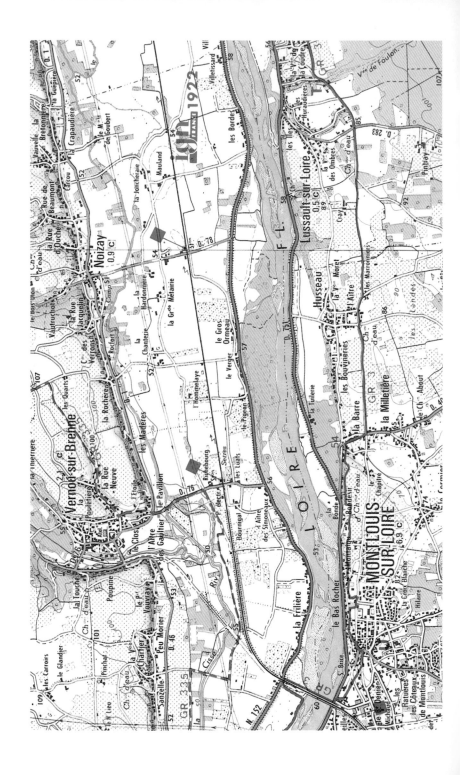

Junction with the D31
Detour *30 mins*
Pagoda of Chantleloup
Chinese tower, remains of château built by the Duke of Choiseul.

5Km
1:15

LUSSAULT-SUR-LOIRE
🏠 🛖 🍴 ⚓ 🚎
(see map ref T)

4Km
1

HUSSEAU-SUR-LOIRE
⚓

5Km
1:15

MONTLOUIS-SUR-LOIRE
🏠 🛖 🍴 🍷 ⚓ 🚌
🚎 ℹ️

(see map ref U)
12th and 16th century church; priest's residence in 16th century mansion.
The town is situated on the edge of the plateau separating the valleys of the Loire and Cher; its renowned white wines are stored in caves cut in the rock.

4Km
1

Junction with GR335
The GR335 links Vouvray and Lavardin.

1Km
0:15

Detour see left. Follow the D31 south as far as the path signposted to the right. You can return to GR3 (spot height 93) along a path leading north from the pagoda.

From the junction with the D31, continue in a south-westerly direction as far as La Richardière (spot height 93). Carry on to Chandon, where you should turn right and then left. Go through L'Ormeau-Vigneau and you will come to the first houses in La Vallée de la Condre on the outskirts of Lussault-sur-Loire.

The GR does not go into Lussault, but carries straight on (south-west) along the same road. It crosses the D283, passes to the south of Cray and takes you through Les Marronniers and L'Aître, to the village of Husseau-sur-Loire.

After L'Aître, the GR3 passes the foot of the water tower. Continue straight on (west) through the vineyards to the junction with the D40 at La Barre. Turn right. Before the crossroads (spot height 54) follow a road to the left for 50 metres and then carry straight on (west) along a path through vineyards. Go through Bondésir and Montaigu. You will come to a cemetery and, following the Chemin de Bellevue, you will reach Montlouis-sur-Loire.

From the church in Montlouis, walk to the mairie; opposite this building, follow a path between two walls and then turn right towards the industrial district and walk as far as the railway bridge over the Loire. The GR crosses the Loire along a pedestrian walkway beside the railway line. Shortly afterwards, turn left on to a dirt track running along the right bank of the river. You will pass the Vouvray camp site. Join the N152 at Les Tuileries, follow it as far as the bridge over the Cisse and turn right on to the earth bank that leads to the junction with the GR335.

At the junction between the GR3 and GR335, the GR3 follows a street (north) as far as a square. Climb a flight of steps leading to the Vouvray church.

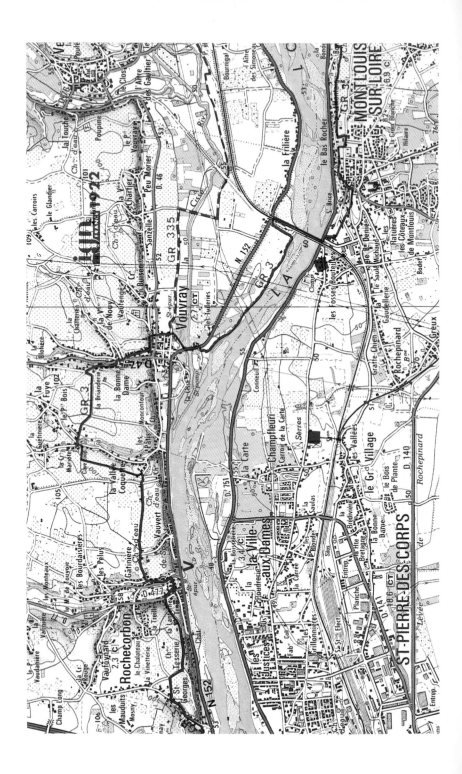

Ronsard

Pierre de Ronsard, 'the gentleman of Vendôme', was born in the manor house of La Possonnière in 1524. Although he spent more time at court than in the Vendôme, he did stay at various places in the valleys of the Loire and the Loir, including the priory of Sainte Madeleine de Croix-Val, where he used to seek relaxation from the 'clamour of the court'. He owned a house in the Vendôme, with a garden bordering the Loir. He also lived at Montoire when he was prior of Saint Gilles at Bourgueil.

It was at the Château of Blois in 1545 that, as a young page of 21, he met the beautiful Cassandra for whom he wrote the one hundred and eighty-three sonnets of 'Les Amours'.

However, it was at the priory of Saint-Côme, which used to stand on an island in the Loire three kilometres from Tours, that he spent the greatest part of his life. This was one of his favourite residences, where he loved to garden and tend flowers and plants. He had become the prior in 1553 and stayed there until his death in 1585.

The priory of Saint-Côme, which was heavily damaged by bombing in 1944, has now been restored and converted. The 12th century refectory and the ruins of the church are open to visitors. The poet's remains are buried near the high altar, under a simple tombstone.

ROGER BEAUMONT

Extract from the article that appeared in the April, 1984 number of *Randonée*, under the title *Musarder avec Ronsard*

VOUVRAY

⌂ 🏕 ✕ 🍷 ⚒ 🚌 🚇 🚏

Troglodyte dwellings and caves cut out of the rock (tufa). The GR3 will take you through vineyards that produce a wine with a fine bouquet. It is said that each glass of Vouvray 'gladdens the heart', and this adage can be confirmed by tasting it.

4Km
1

From the Place de l'Eglise in Vouvray, walk to the top of the hill through the hamlet of La Bonne Dame where there are cellars in which the wine-growers of La Chantepleure hold meetings and celebratioins. Cross the D47 and continue as far as the Brianderie cross-roads; turn left and follow the road (south-west, then west) to La Croix-Mariote. Follow the road south for 100 metres and continue (west then south) on a path that leads through the vineyard. You will come to La Vallée Coquette. Skirt left round the hamlet and continue in a westerly direction through the vineyards as far as La Gâtinière crossroads, close to Rochecorbon.

ROCHECORBON

⌂ 🏕 ✕ 🍷 ⚒ 🚌 🚇

*(see map ref V)
13th century church, remodelled in the 16th century; La Lanterne (15th century lookout tower).*

6Km
1:30

At La Gâtinière crossroads, the GR3 turns left (south). Follow this road for 250 metres, turn right (north) and then bear west towards La Lanterne. Carry on through the vineyards to Saint-Georges. Go through Les Rochettes and bear left (south-west), skirting the Abbey of Marmoutier, to the N152. Cross the N152, opposite the entrance to the abbey, and follow

85

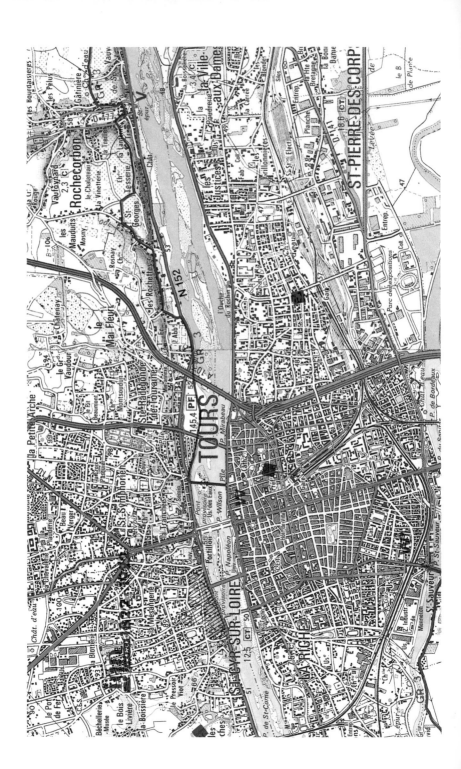

From vine to wine
Established in 1975 in the ancient cellars of the Abbaye Saint-Julien in Tours, the Museum of Touraine Wines is an eloquent witness to the history, origins and folklore of wine-growing. It is a rich source of information on the still-continuing activity of the wine growers' brotherhoods, on wine-growing itself and on the trades and professions linked, more or less closely, to the prosperity of a type of agriculture to which the province owes some of its prestige. Another wine museum has opened at Chevrette (2 kilometres from Bourgueil), not far from an old quarry that now serves as a wine-tasting cellar. There are a host of collective wine stores and co-operative cellars, both in the valley of the Cher and in the vineyards of Chinon and Vouvray.

The Touraine vineyards are very old: legend has it that Saint Martin's ass (4th century) made those in Vouvray fertile by grazing on them. There are several qualities of wine. The product of the best grape variety is the Pineau de Loire, or Chenin. Celebrated by Rabelais, Chinon wine, with its taste of raspberries, is aged in cellars carved out of the local tufa. Nowadays, there are very few farms that do not give at least a patch of land to vines, or a row of vines with a good aspect, to make wine for family consumption. The good, and long-established, local vines are blended with more productive varieties, to produce wine for 'everyday drinking'.

All Touraine wines are AOC wines (appellation d'origine contrôlée), while the good-quality wines are labelled simply 'appellation Touraine'.
BERNARD HENNEQUIN

TOURS
🏛 🏠 ⛺ 🍴 🍷 ⚓
🚌 🚃 🛈

Capital of the Touraine originally occupied by a Gallic tribe (the Turonnes); became the capital of the third 'Lyonnaise' (one of the divisions of Roman Gaul) before Saint-Martin made it an important Christian centre. Place Plumereau (15th century); Cathedral of Saint-Gatien (13th and 16th centuries); Saint Martin's Basilica; Charlemagne' tower; churches; cloisters;

8Km
2

a path that runs between the Loire and the camp site. Walk under the motorway bridge and continue along the Loire to the bridge reserved for pedestrians and cyclists. Cross over and walk into the city of Tours.

The GR3 is not signposted across the city; the signs start again at the Saint-Sauveur bridge over the Cher (see map ref W) at the junction of the GR3, which heads west, and the GR46, which leads east.

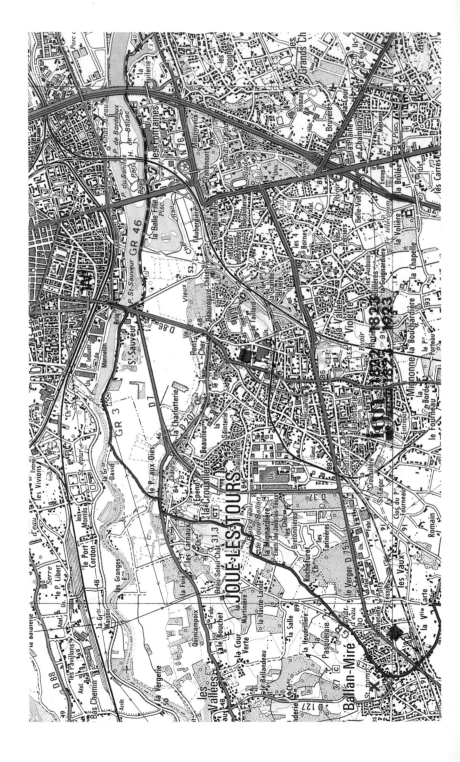

Cutting tufa

Stone-cutters from regions other than Anjou and Touraine do not find tufa an easy stone to work with. How often one hears curses hurled at the stone. Some people even go so far as to say that tufa is not stone; it must be said that a lot of local people think the same thing: watching us work, they often ask, 'Is that stone or tufa?'. This always raises a smile, because tufa is, of course, a stone, but what kind of stone exactly?

Tufa is a stone that is classified as very soft, probably the softest there is. But soft does not mean easy to work with. A lot of precautions have to be taken when it is being cut. For stone-cutters used to a harder, firmer material, the fragility of tufa is disconcerting. Handling it during the cutting process requires great care. Mere finger pressure on the ridges and edges is sufficient to make them crumble, and the careless use of a tool causes fragments to chip off. This difficulty is compounded by the presence in the rock of very hard clumps of iron ore. Cutting these hard clumps, fused into a soft material, can very easily cause part of the material to be torn away, leaving holes in the stone.

If the stone-cutter finds his initial contact with tufa disheartening, this situation does not last for a long time. After a while, when he has had time to get to know his material and to master it, he ends up liking it, since tufa also has some good qualities. Apart from the clumps of iron ore, its delicacy means it can be carved into some beautiful shapes, and the eye never tires of its beautiful, light yellow ochre colour and its velvety appearance.

A stone-cutter's kit contains many different tools. Each grade of stone, classified by hardness (granite, marble, cold stone, hard, semi-hard and firm stone) has its own set of tools.

Extract from the magazine Le Pays d'Anjou

museums of Fine Arts and of Trade-Guilds; Gemmail Museum; cellier Saint-Julien, etc. . . . .
In surrounding area: Château de Plessis-les-Tours where Louis XI lived; priory of Saint-Cosme, where visitors will find memories of Ronsard.

BALLAN-MIRÉ

(see map ref X)
12th century church – 16th century stained-glass windows.

In Tours, turn right (west) just after the Saint-Sauveur bridge into the Rue du Pont-aux-Oies and walk along the left bank of the Cher. At a fork before La Grange-David, turn left and cross over the Vieux-Cher on the Pont-aux-Oies. Turn right after the bridge on to the D207 and then turn left at the first crossroads (south); follow the road as far as the lake at Joué-Ballan. Walk through La Mignardière and Rochefuret and across two crossroads before coming to Ballan-Miré.

East of the church in Ballan-Miré follow the D127 (south-east) crossing the D751 and carry on as far as the Vieille-Carte crossroads. Bear right (south) and skirt the wall of the Château de la Carte. Pass close to Le Grand-Porteau and turn right to the west of Le Larvoir. At the crossroads (spot height 94) follow the road to the right (south-west) as far as La Ferronnerie.

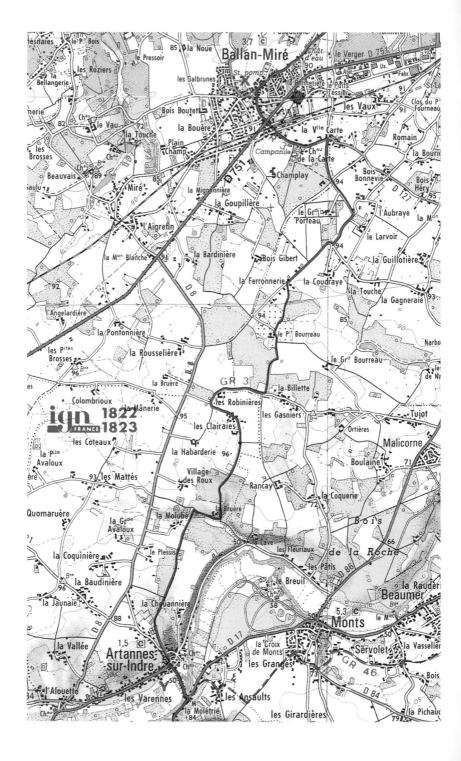

10Km
2:30

At this point, the GR takes a path that leads south to Le Petit-Bourreau and carries on in the same direction to the outskirts of La Billette, where it joins a road. Bear right and pass Les Robinières; shortly afterwards, follow the road east as far as Les Clairaies, then head across fields and through woods to La Bruère; at the hamlet, turn right (west) and, 500 metres further on, carry on along a path (south-west) that will take you to the east of La Molubé. The path continues, either through undergrowth or along the edge of woods, to the cemetery and the market town of Artannes-sur-Indre.

ARTANNES-SUR-INDRE
🏠 Å ✕ ♆ ♨ ☷

5Km
0:10
(see map ref Y)
16th century château; 12th and 15th century church.

In Artannes, follow the D17 (south-east) and cross the Indre. You will come to the mill of La Molétrie.

Junction with GR46

2.5Km
0:35

From la Molétrie mill, the GR3 follows the road along the Indre (south-west), goes through Le Haut-Village and Potard and comes to Pont-de-Ruan.

PONT-DE-RUAN
🏠 ✕ ♆ ♨ ☷
10th and 12th century

From Pont-de-Ruan, the GR continues south-west along the D17 to the Croix-Billette crossroads; here, turn right on to the path that

Balzac's house at Saché

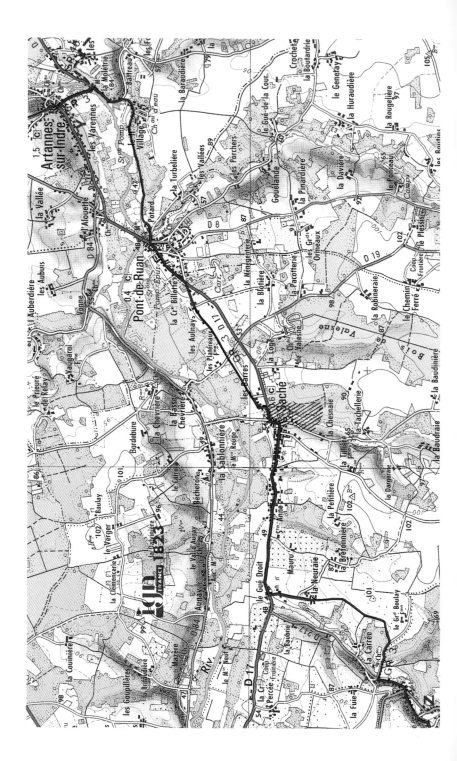

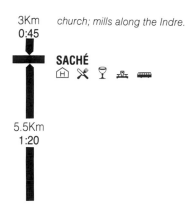

3Km
0:45

church; mills along the Indre.

SACHÉ

5.5Km
1:20

takes you through Les Aulnays and Les Barres into Saché.

From the church in Saché, follow the D17 west as far as Le Gué-Droit. Do not cross the river, but turn left (south) and follow the road as far as La Neuraie. Continue straight on along a path until you come to a small road; here, bear right and skirt the grounds of the Château La Carrée until you come to the D217, which you will follow (south-west) as far as a crossroads (spot height 61). Continue straight on to the hamlet of La Vallée.

Balzac and the Touraine

'**D**o not ask me why I love the Touraine. I do not love it as one loves one's birthplace, nor as one loves an oasis in the desert; I love it as an artist loves art; I love it less than I love you, but without the Touraine, perhaps I would no longer be alive.'

Balzac was born in Tours in 1799 and remained deeply attached to his native province, which provided the background for a great deal of his work. Saché was the place he preferred to stay. It was in the château (where today a museum is devoted to the writer) that he wrote or planned part of his work, particularly 'Le lys dans la vallée'. The mills on the Indre at Pont-de-Ruan are evocative of his description of them in that book.

'Imagine three mills standing among gracefully irregular islands surmounted by a few clumps of trees in the middle of a field of water; how else is it possible to describe those robust, colourful aquatic plants that carpet the river, rise above it, undulate with it, surrender themselves to its whims and bend with the turbulance of the river as it is pounded by the mill wheels!

Here and there rise mounds of gravel on which the water breaks, forming a border on which the sun glints. Amaryllises, water lillies, rushes and phlox decorate the banks with their magnificent tapestries. A rickety bridge made of rotten planks, its supports covered with flowers and its rails veiled in hardy grasses and velvety mosses, leans over the river yet does not fall; dilapidated boats, fishermen's nets, the monotonous song of a shepherd, ducks swimming between the islands or cleaning themselves on the coarse sand brought down by the river; mill-hands, their caps over their ears, busy loading their mules; each of these details bestowed a surprising naïvety on the scene. Imagine, beyond the bridge, two or three farms, a dovecote, some turtle-doves, about thirty tumbledown cottages separated by gardens, hedges of honeysuckle, jasmine and clematis; then a dung heap in front of every door, and chickens and roosters on the paths. That is the village of Pont-de-Ruan, a pretty village surmounted by an old church of great character, a church dating from the time of the crusades, like those painters seek for their pictures.'

HONORÉ DE BALZAC

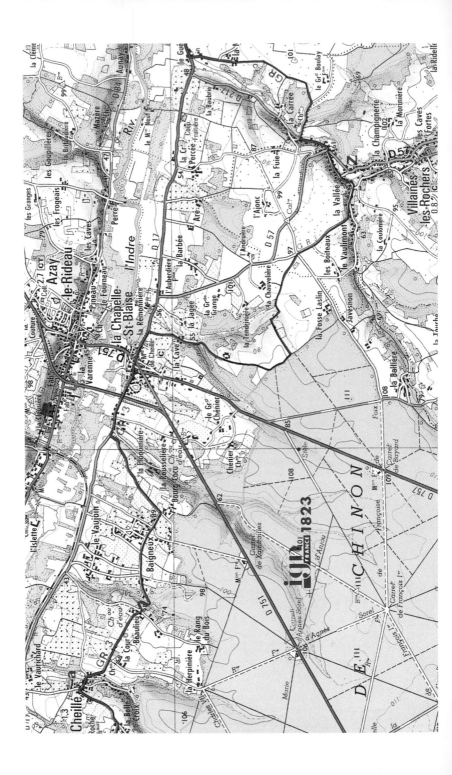

La Vallée
(see map ref Z)
Detour *15 mins*
VILLAINE-LES-ROCHERS
🏠 𝕏 ✕ ⅄ ⚒ ▭
5.5Km   *Pretty basket makers'*
1:25   *village; centre for*
wickerwork.
Follow the D57 in a southerly
direction.

**LA CHAPELLE-SAINT-
BLAISE**
🏠 ✕ ⅄ ⚒ ▭
Detour *15 mins*
AZAY-LE-RIDEAU
🏠 𝕏 ✕ ⅄ ⚒ 🚌
5Km   ▭ 🅱
1:15
Renaissance château
surrounded by the Indre
(son et lumière in season);
church of Saint-Symphorien
(9th and 10th centuries).
Follow the D751 (north)
across the Indre.

CHEILLÉ
⚒
(see map ref a)
13th century church.

From La Vallée, follow the road (west, then north-west) to a crossroads (spot height 97); leave the road to the left and follow the path (north-west). After a winding stretch, this will bring you to the forest of Chinon. On the edge of the forest, turn right on to a path skirting the trees (north west, then north). When you come to La Cave and the D17, bear left (north-west) and walk into La Chapelle-Saint-Blaise.

In La Chapelle-Saint-Blaise, the GR3 continues along the D17 (north-west) for 1 kilometre. Turn left along the road leading to Bourg-Cocu; there, bear right and walk through Baigneux and Beaulieu. After passing the Château de la Cour you will come to Cheillé.

From Cheillé, the GR3 leads past the church. At the first crossroads, follow the road on the left as far as La Belle-Croix and you will come (west) to the edge of the forest of Chinon.

The Château at La Chapelle-Saint-Blaise

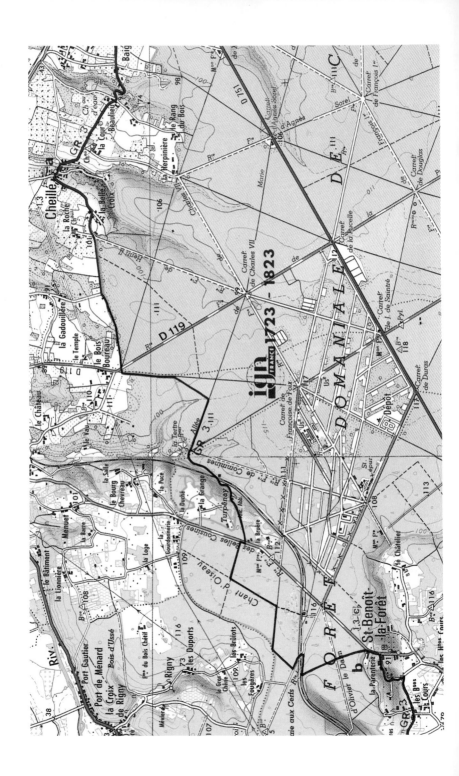

Continue as far as the D119 to the south of Le Bois-Bourreau. Cross this road and enter the wood along a path (south) leading to the Allée de Marie-d'Anjou; turn right, and at the end of the track take the winding path facing you (south-west) that crosses the railway at a level crossing. You will pass close to the Abbey of Turpênay.

Skirt round the Abbey of Turpênay and follow the path leading to the forest track of Les Belles-Cousines; cross the track and follow a forest path almost opposite you (slightly to the right) for 500 metres as far as a crossroads at Chant d'Oiseau. Bear left; after 750 metres, turn right for 500 metres and join a track leading to the Duras forest trail; turn left on to this trail. Cross the railway and turn right on to the path behind the gate-keeper's garden; follow it for 250 metres and carry on to the left (south-east) along a straight path leading to the Belles-Cousines forest trail. You will come to Saint-Benoît-la-Forêt.

10Km
2:30

SAINT-BENOÎT-LA-FORÊT
🏕 🍴 ⚓ ════
(see map ref b)

Before the market town of Saint-Benoît-la-Forêt, the GR3 turns right to La Parenterie. The footpath then turns left down a shaded alley, lined with wine cellars. Take the path to the right of a bridge and walk as far as Les Basses-Cours. Follow the path (west then south-west) leading to the Jacques-Molay forester's lodge. Carry straight on (south-west) along the Rabelais forest track as far as the Charles le Téméraire crossroads. Take the second path on the left (south), the Allée de Louis XI. The GR does not go as far as the forester's lodge, but turns right slightly before it (south-east) and crosses a small road before coming to Rochambeau-Village on the edge of the forest. Follow the road to the left (south-east) as far as the D751 (see map ref c). Cross this road and carry on into the industrial district. The path continues south into some woods and ends up at a road junction. Follow the path that takes you south of Bel-Air and walk west along a path overlooking the River Vienne past the ruins of the chapelle Sainte-Radegonde. This will bring you close to the Château of Chinon.

12Km
3

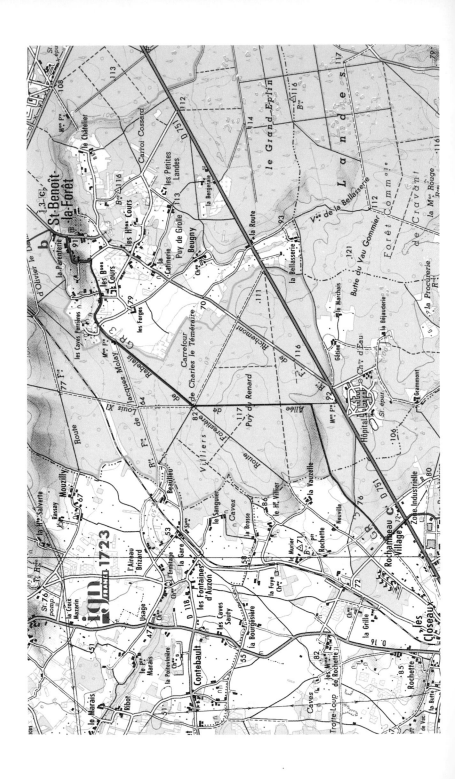

CHINON

Ⓗ ⌂ Å ✕ ⲩ ⚓
✇ ▭ ⓲

*Historic site since time of
Romans; the writer Rabelais
is associated with the town.
The area produces a famous
red wine.
Fortified castle; house of the
States General; church of
Saint-Etienne (15th century);
church of Saint-Maurice
(12th century nave) in
Angevin style; Grand-Carroi
(museum of historic
Chinon); bridge over the
Vienne (12th century).*

**10Km
2:30**

The GR3 passes fairly close to the Chinon castle and then follows the Rue Jeanne d'Arc as far as Le Grand-Carroi. Cross the bridge over the Vienne and turn right (west) on to the road that runs along the river. You will pass through Sauvegrain and Pontille; after Les Granges, the road gives way to a path that follows the route of an old Roman road. The footpath passes the Île à Seguin (see map ref d) and joins the D751 on the edge of La Chaussée.

Detour *20 mins*
LA ROCHELLE
⌂

*Follow the small routes that
lead north-west through the
vineyards towards Les
Quinquenets and La
Rochelle.*

LA CHAUSSÉE
Ⓗ Å ✕ ⲩ ⚓ ▭

On the edge of La Chaussée, turn right on to the D751, follow it for 100 metres and then turn

---

Rabelais

It would be impossible to linger in the Touraine without pursuing the memory of Rabelais and his progeny of good-natured, gluttonous giants. Some claim to see in Rabelais the most perfect incarnation of the national genius, putting him in the same position as Shakespeare in England and Cervantes in Spain. Much of his epic, picaresque fresco unfolds in the places he frequented as a child, on the left bank of the Vienne, opposite Chinon. There, around his birthplace of La Devinière and the Châteaux of Maulévrier and Le Coudray-Montpensier, blows were exchanged in the Picrocholean Wars, which started as a result of an altercation between the cake-bakers of Lerné and the shepherds of Seuilly. At the Benedictine abbey of Seuilly, where the young Rabelais received his classical education, Friar John of the Hashes, 'a tall, thin fellow with a great gaping mouth and a fine outstanding nose, a grand mumbler of matins, dispatcher of masses and polisher off of vigils', drove the people of Lerné out of the abbey vineyard by attacking them with the staff of his processional cross. And at La Roche-Clermault, Gargantua led the forces that recaptured Grandgousier's castle.

PHILIPPE LEVÉE

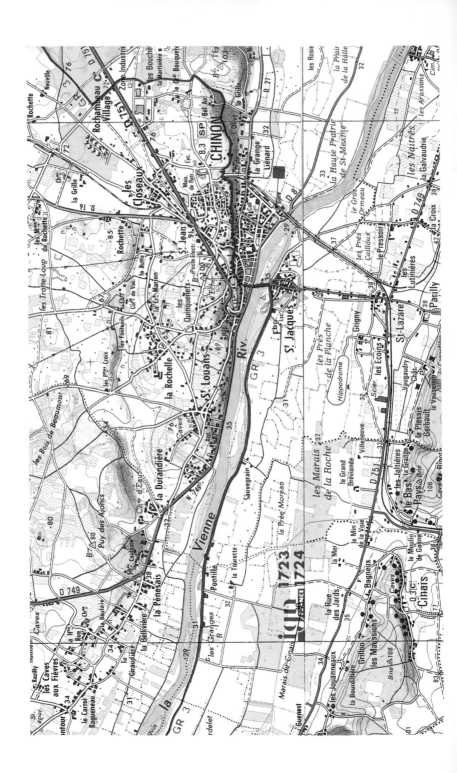

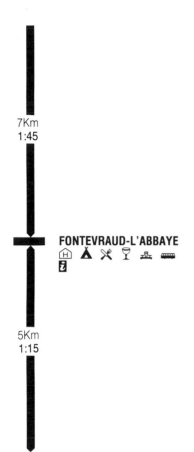

7Km
1:45

FONTEVRAUD-L'ABBAYE

5Km
1:15

left on to a path that leads up the hill. At the top of the hill, turn right off the minor road on to a path leading through orchards and vineyards; follow it as far as La Vallée des Veaux, from where you can see the Château of Petit-Thouars to the north. Turn left (south-west) into the hamlet and carry on to the edge of the forest of Fontevrault at the place known as l'Etang. Follow the forest track (west) and you will come to a road leading to La Vallée-de-Crotte. Ignore this road (keeping it on your right) and continue straight on. Cross the road to La Roncheraie and carry on into the forest. After the chapel of Notre-Dame-de-Pitié, take the street leading into Fontevraud-l'Abbaye.

In Fontevraud-l'Abbaye, the GR3 follows the main road past the abbey. It takes the road to Montsoreau, turns into the second road on the right and follows a path leading up into the wood. Turn left into the wood (spot height 102) and follow the path (north) until it meets a small road; here, bear right (east) into a hollow in the ground. At a crossroads, take the second road on the left leading to Candes-Saint-Martin. Before the village, turn right and walk up to the ruins of an old mill (panoramic view of the confluence of the Vienne and Loire, and the Chinon nuclear power station). Follow a fairly steep path downhill into Candes-Saint-Martin.

Fontrevaud
The famous Abbey of Fontevraud was founded by Robert d'Arbrissel at the beginning of the 12th century, in the middle of a forest that was then much larger. From the very beginning, this order was very successful, and both men and women gathered around Robert d'Arbrisse. Postulants arrived in their thousands. By 1245 the order numbered almost 5,000 members. Work on the abbey church began in 1102 and it was consecrated by Pope Calixtus II. It is the most northerly church with a cupola. The choir houses the tombs of Plantagenet sovereigns, Henry II, Richard the Lionheart, Eleanor of Aquitaine and Isabelle of Angoulême.
For 150 years, Fontevraud was used as a prison before becoming the Cultural Centre of the West in 1975. The abbey, which is being restored, has found a new vocation as a regional, national and international meeting place with a full programme of cultural events.

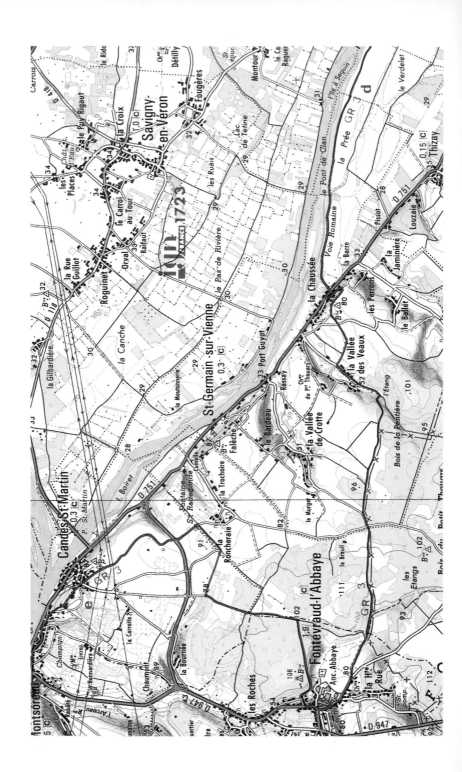

CANDES-SAINT-MARTIN

🏕 ✕ ⚓

(see map ref C)
12th and 13th century
church, fortified in 15th
century, stands on site of
cell where Saint Martin died
in 397. Chinon is renowned
for its white wines.

2Km
0:30

From the southern edge of Candes-Saint-Martin, the GR3 continues in a north-westerly direction. The path joins a road leading behind the chateau to the church of Montsoreau.

MONTSOREAU

🏠 🏕 ✕ 🅱

15th and 16th century
houses, 15th century
château. Also renowned for
its white wines.

3Km
0:45

From the church in Montsoreau, take the first street on the left (south-west), then first right towards the water tower, which you will pass. Bear right into the vineyards on to the road to La Vignole; turn left and follow the road lined with wine cellars. Skirt round the grounds of the château and you will come to the church of Turquant.

TURQUANT

🍷 ▭ ⚓

15th century church.

From the church in Turquant, follow the road (north-west) to Le Val Hulin. At the first junction, bear left (south) and follow the path through the vineyards until you come to a minor road, on to which you turn right (south-

---

Candes Saint-Martin Montsoreau

It is virtually impossible to separate these two villages of Candes and Montsoreau.

Candes, which means 'confluence', is aptly named, since it overlooks the confluence of the Loire and the Vienne which forms a huge stretch of water. Time has virtually stood still in these villages on the banks of the Loire, where many examples of the regional architecture are to be seen (Romanesque, Gothic and Renaissance). The Romanesque church of Candes, which dates from the 12th and 13th centuries, contains the remains of Saint Martin, evangelist and Bishop of Tours. The body of Saint Martin, kept by the people of Poitou, was seized by the monks of Tours.

Montsoreau was an important port on the Loire. In the days when lighters plied the Loire, the port handled agricultural products and wine from northern Poitou and the Chinon region as well as tufa, the local stone.

The village encircles the 15th century château, (the residence of Charles de Chambres, who carried out the massacres of Saint Bartholomew's Day in Anjou), which overlooks the Loire. Part fortress, part residence, the château in which Henry IV lived now houses the Musée des Goums (museum of Moroccan troops in the French army), which was transferred from Rabat in 1956. Among the old houses in Montsoreau is the residence of 'la Dame de Montsoreau', the wife of Charles de Chambres and heroine of Alexandre Dumas's novel of the same name.

The building currently houses exhibitions of paintings.

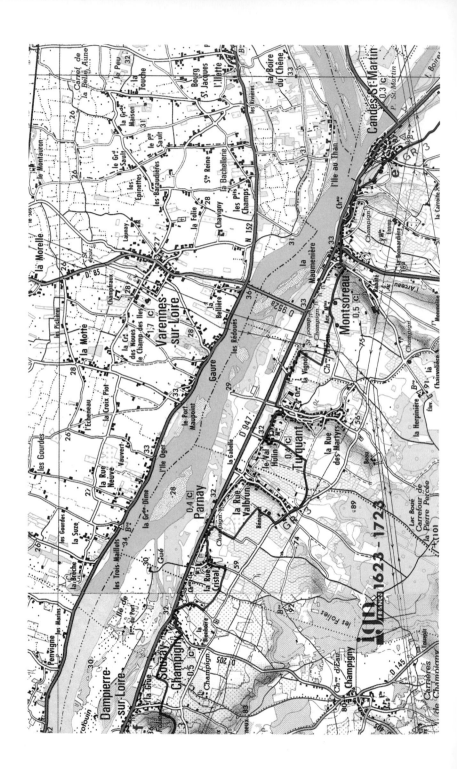

3Km
0:45

PARNAY
🏠 ✕ 🍷 🚉 🚌
Church of Saint-Pierre:
Romanesque nave, 15th
century apse, Renaissance
portal.

1.5Km
0:20

SOUZAY-CHAMPIGNY
🍷 🚉
15th and 16th century
buildings; restored manor
house, where Margaret of
Anjou, daughter of King
René and wife of Henry V of
England, died in 1482;
church of Saint-Maurice
(15th century). Renowned
for its red wines.

3Km
0:45

DAMPIERRE-SUR-LOIRE
⛺ 🍷 🚉 🚌
(see map ref f)
Troglodyte houses;
Renaissance houses; caves
in the rock.

2.5Km
0:40

Junction with the GR36
The GR36 heads south
towards Montreuil-Bellay and
Parthenay.
The GR3 and GR36 follow
the same route north-west
as far as Saumur.

1.5Km
0:25

Saumur

west). Cross the road leading to La Rue Valbrun. Then take the path on the right leading to the old Béniquet mill; from there, follow a path on the left through vineyards and turn right (north) on to a road that will bring you down to Parnay.

From the church in Parnay, follow a path that forks to the left and leads to the Rue Cristal. In the hamlet, walk in a southerly direction. Take a path on the right, bordered by walls, and head in a westerly then north-westerly direction through vineyards to the church of Souzay-Champigny.

The GR3 takes you close to the church of Souzay-Champigny and then joins D947, only to leave it immediately as it turns left. As you leave the village you will see an old mill. Turn right on to the path that winds through the vineyards. Cross the road to Dampierre and walk round the Butte de la Folie to the south and west and into the village of Dampierre-sur-Loire.

From Dampierre-sur-Loire, go up a narrow street to the left behind the church. At the crossroads, before the cemetery, turn right (north-east then north-west) into an alley between old walls. Go through the Bizeau vineyard and walk to Beaulieu. Turn left (south-west) and walk as far as Le Tyreau. Turn right (north-west) on to a path between vineyards and woods; follow a small road that will take you to the north of a water tower and then to the D145.

The GR3 and GR36 continue north-west along the D145 (Rue des Moulins), and take you to a car park near the Château of Saumur.

The footpaths GR3 and GR36 are not signposted through the town. The continuation of the GR3 to Guérande is given in the following

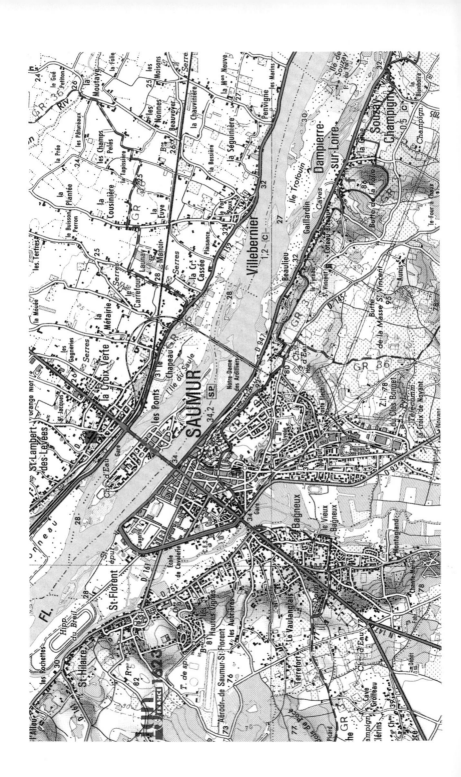

Detour *30 mins*
Saumur station

walk. The following detour will take you to Saumur station.

Detour see left. The station is on the right bank of the Loire. From the car park at the Château de Saumur, follow the Avenue du Docteur-Perron, the Grand'Rue, the Place Saint-Pierre, the Rue de la Tonnelle and walk past the Town Hall to the Loire. Cross the Pont Cessart and the Pont des Cadets, then turn left towards the station.

Saumur and the horse

The château, massive and compact, but with a certain grace imparted by the vertical lines of its towers, was rebuilt on the site of an ancient fortress built by Foulques Nerra. Today it houses the Equestrian Museum. Among other things, it contains the skeleton of Flying Fox, the god-like stallion, sold for half a million francs half a century ago. This horse earned his owner 50,000 francs every time he was used for stud. He died in 1911 at the age of 15 while performing his duties!

Everything here is surprising. There is a print depicting an orchestra playing in the Saumur riding school for the animals to dance to! The visitor can also see remains of prehistoric horses, a portrait of the first French horse to win the Epsom Derby, a collection of stirrups, some fitted with foot-warmers, and this quotation from Mohammed:
You will be the lord of all animals
And men will follow you everywhere you go.
ARMAND LANOUX

WALK 3

SAUMUR

🏨 ⌂ ⚓ ✕ ♉ ⚒
🚍 🚃 ℤ

Château, ancient fortress built in 10th, and rebuilt in 14th and 16th centuries; 16th century Hôtel de Ville (town hall); church of Saint-Pierre, built in the Angevin style; church of Notre-Dame-de-Nantilly; Equestrian Museum; Museum of Decorative Arts; Cavalry School; Armoured Corps Museum.

1Km
0:20

BAGNEUX

✕ ⚒

The largest dolmen in Europe stands in the courtyard of the café Grand Dolmen. Ask the proprietor for permission to see it.

5Km
1:15

Marson

The hamlet of Rou Marson is composed of troglodytic dwellings. On your way along the GR3 you will have seen some dug out of the tufa cliff between Montsoreau and Saumur. Further on you will find more such dwellings, but of a different type, the so-called 'cave dwellings'. In Anjou, east of a line drawn north-south through Angers, two types of troglodytic dwellings are found: those with mullion windows dug out of the

4Km
1

The walk begins at the Saumur railway station on the right bank of the river. The GR3 is not signposted through the town. Turn right on leaving the station. Cross two bridges over the Loire, the Pont des Cadets and the Pont Cessart. Carry straight on through the Place Bilange, Rue Roosevelt, Rue d'Orléans, Rue Maréchal Leclerc and Rue du Général Leclerc as far as the next bridge, the Pont Fouchard. The GR3 heads towards Nantes from the Pont-Fouchard, on the River Thouet, south-west of Saumur. Having crossed the bridge, turn left on to the footpath along the Avenue des Peupleraies. After about 300 metres, turn left on to a tarmac path with walls on either side that leads up to the Rue Desmaret, which you should go along.

At the café Grand Dolmen take the Rue de l'Arche almost opposite and cross the N147. Then take the Rue de la Bergère to the cemetery and turn left, cross a road and follow a road opposite you for 2 kilometres. This road becomes a path, skirts Pocé wood, crosses a road and goes down into Riou. The GR turns right and wends its way roads lined with troglodytic dwellings to the D305, which will lead you into Marson.

At the church, turn left and continue along the D305 for 500 metres. At the end of the wall surrounding the grounds of the château, turn right on to a path leading along the edge of Marson pond and then up into the wood. Caution: about 1 kilometre from the pond, the forest trail comes to a fire-break and 100 metres further on, the GR turns left on to a path leading downhill out of the wood. If you follow some wide paths used to link plots of land, you will come to the D161; cross it and enter Villemolle.

hillside in the Saumurois and, dwellings dug out of the open countryside in the region of Doué-la-Fontaine.

Villemolle

2Km
0:30

Walk through the hamlet. At the crossroads (spot height 89), turn left (north-west) on to a path leading towards a wood. A few metres after you enter this wood, the GR turns left on to a path leading to a wide avenue. Turn right on to it and continue to the hamlet of La Croix.

La Croix

3Km
0:45

Follow the road on the left for 350 metres and turn right on to another road that leads towards the Château de Sainte-Radegonde. At La Gilberderie, the GR3 turns left along an orchard on to a path which, after 1 kilometre, joins a road. Turn right on to it and follow it as it winds its way down into Chênehutte-les-Truffeaux.

CHÊNEHUTTE-LES-TRUFFEAUX

3.5Km
0:55

This place is called Chênehutte-les-Truffeaux because of the many stone quarries that are now used for the cultivation of mushrooms; along the hillside, the GR3 passes close to a Roman camp known as 'le châtelier'. The church in Chênehutte dates from the 11th century.

Turn left on to the D751 for a few metres. Cross the little bridge over the stream of Fontaine de l'Enfer and turn immediately left into the road running alongside it. Follow it for 300 metres, then turn right onto a steep path that will take you close to the Roman camp. Take a road to the left that goes past some bungalows, a farm and a shooting ground; 1 kilometre further on, at the crossroads, turn right on to another road bordered by woods then fields. You will come to a junction.

Junction
Detour *20 mins*
la Métairie farm
Riding centre; basic shelter with showers and lavatories.

1.5Km
0:20

Detour see left. Turn left and follow the road as far as the crossroads known as La Croix de Cunault. Here turn left on to another road leading to La Métairie.

The GR3 then goes downhill to the right along a sunken road leading to Trévées.

TRÈVES

16th century manor house of

The GR goes through the village along minor roads lined with walls. Beside the tower of Trèves, turn left up a minor road that leads

111

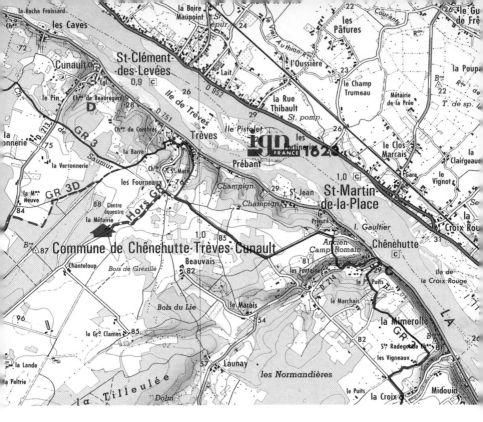

0.7Km 0:10	*La Cour Condé; 11th and 12th century church; 15th century keep.*	back to the plateau. After La Barre, bear right and walk to the Saumur road, which is the junction with the GR3D. For the alternative route see page 127.
	Junction with the GR3D **Detour** *20 mins* **Cunault** *Prior's house, 16th century; Château de Cunault, 19th century; portal, 17th century; Château de la Roche-Froissard and Château de Beauregard;*	
6Km 1:30	*church with 11th century belfry which, since 1966, has housed four bells from Constantine cathedral; 12th century church of Saint-Maxenceul.* *Turn right and follow the D213 into the village.*	The GR3 turns right on to the path known as the Saumur road. 1 kilometre further on you will cross the D213.

The GR3 continues along the Saumur road and 700 metres after crossing the D213, turns left on to a forest path that leads to Cunault pond. At the crossroads after the pond, it turns right into a wide forest avenue which leads back to the Saumur road. Turn left on to this path which joins the road leading to Gennes.

GENNES

⌂ 𝐀 ✕ ⚓ 🚌 ℹ

The Church of Saint-Vétérin dates from the 10th and 15th centuries; 12th century belfry of Saint-Eusèbe.

2Km
0:30

Opposite the car park, beside the Maison Familiale, the GR3 goes up the Rue de la Montée des Juifs to the belfry of Saint-Eusèbe.

It then follows the Rue du Mémorial, crosses the D70 and goes up towards the woods. Take the first path on the right and walk down to La Pagerie.

La Pagerie

Not marked on the 1:50,000 map.

4Km
1

Detour *20 mins*
Saint-Pierre-en-Vaux
Continue straight on following the signposted diversion.

After La Pagerie, turn right to walk up a broad path that passes close to the *dolmen*. When you leave the wood, turn right and cross the plateau, passing close to a ruined mill. Do not follow the road that goes down to Nidevelle, but turn left (south-west) and, 300 metres further on, you will come to a crossroads.

The GR3 turns right on to a path through the wood that leads to the agricultural college near the church of Saint-Georges-des-Sept-Voies.

Saint-Georges-des-Sept-Voies

Romanesque church. Orme de Sully.

At the crossroads at the church, the GR3 turns right, skirts the cemetery and joins the D156 which it follows as far as the next crossroads.

Alternative route to Cumeray via the hamlets of Nideville and Salle Village. Take the road on the right at the crossroads.

3Km
0:45

Continuing along the D156, the GR3 passes close to a wayside shrine; 250 metres further on, turn left (north-west) on to a path through the woods which bends to the right and leads to the D751. Take a minor road opposite you and, 100 metres afer a left-hand bend, ignore the road to the right (east) and take a path that crosses the D156 and then leads to Cumeray. (On the right you will rejoin the alternative route from Nideville).

Cumeray

The GR3 bears left (north) into a narrow street

2Km
0:25

LE THOUREIL
✗ ▥

*Former port on the Loire.
Short circular walk.*

3Km
0:45

ABBEY OF SAINT-MAUR
⌂

*Abbey founded in the 6th
century and now used as a
meeting centre.*

3Km
0:40

Detour
*A little way down the hill, on
the right, there is a
panoramic view over the
Loire.*

**SAINT-RÉMY-LA-
VARENNE**
▲ ✗ ⚓ ▥

*12th and 13th century
church; 13th century priory.
Short-distance footpath.*

2Km
0:30

in the hamlet and continues along a tarmac path skirting the boundary wall of an estate. Continue north-north-east up a wooded hill, then walk down towards le Thoreil. The GR3 turns left 100 metres before the Loire and goes up a narrow path parallel to the river, passing behind the village of Le Thoureil.

Leave Le Thoureil in a north-north-westerly direction towards some woods. A wide path leads through the woods, and, after 2 kilometres, joins a road. Turn right and follow it downhill for 250 metres. The abbey is 100 metres further along this road, just off the GR.

The GR3 leaves the road, takes a path on the left and, 200 metres further on, after passing the old lime kilns, turns right on to a forest trail which, 500 metres further on, comes to a crossroads. The GR continues straight on to the hamlet of Boissay.

From Boissay, the GR3 goes down the road for 500 metres and turns left near a house on to a path that takes you near to the cemetery of Saint-Rémy-la-Varenne.

The GR crosses D21 before the cemetery and continues along the same path which turns left and crosses a small stream. Cross the D55 and take the path opposite leading up into the woods. It passes some distance from the Perchard farm and heads in a westerly direction towards Chauvigné before coming to a road. Turn left on to this road and follow it for 200 metres; turn right into an alleyway between some houses and walk to Chauvigné.

Abbey of Saint-Maur
Founded by Saint Maur in the 6th century, the abbey was destroyed by the Normans and fortified during the Hundred Years' War. Of particular note is the Cross of Saint Maur, composed of five stones inserted into an 11th century wall that was once part of the façade of the abbey church built at the end of the 10th and beginning of the 11th centuries by monks returning to Glanfeuil after the Norman invasion and the transference of the remains of Saint Maur to Saint-Pierre-des-Fossés.

Chauvigné
Fine houses.

4Km
1

BLAISON
🍴 🍷 ⛲ 🚌

Walk down to the right for 200 metres and turn left (west) on to a path linking plots of land. After 300 metres you will have an extensive view over the Loire. Continue towards the wood and turn left on to a path along the edge of the wood leading to the Blaison road. Turn right on to it and walk past Les Granges and round the mills of Blaison until you come to D128, near the cemetery and village of Blaison.

The GR3 does not go into the village, but crosses the D128 and continues for 100 metres before turning left (due south) on to a path that leads behind the grounds of the

6.5Km
1:40

Detour *10 mins*
LE BOIS BRAINSON

Château de la Giraudière. At La Croix de Pissot, cross the road and, 250 metres further on, turn right on to a sunken path. It bends to the left. Without going to Le Coquereau, the GR3 turns left towards the D55 and then turns right on to a path leading to Le Haut-Chemant. The GR goes through the hamlet and, 500 metres further on, turns left and then immediately right.

The GR continues on this road for 500 metres and then turns left (west) on to a path leading to l'Aireau. As it leaves the hamlet, the path bears left. Further on 150 metres, turn right off it towards the wall of the Château d'Ambroise.

1Km
0:15

SAINT-SATURNIN

SAINT-JEAN-DES-MAUVRETS

Old houses.

JUIGNÉ-SUR-LOIRE

Assumed site of battle between Crassus and Dumna in 52 BC; Villa on royal estates in 9th century. Parish in 10th century. Slate workings from 12th century onwards. Ancient Roman embankment destroyed by the Loire and Louet, remains visible at low water.

From here, walkers can take the city bus service into Angers.

ERIGNÉ

Château du Jau and Château de Saint-Pierre. 15th, 16th and 18th century church.

On top of the cliff is a

Turn left and, 100 metres further on, the GR bears right, crosses a meadow and skirts the wall of the estate. Cross the road and continue straight on in a westerly direction as far as the next road, opposite a restored manor house. Turn right along this road and turn off it after 200 metres on to a path leading to Saint-Saturnin.

In the Place de l'Eglise, go down a small road which turns left; the GR3 leaves the road at the next bend for a sunken path leading between walls to Saint-Jean-des-Mauvrets. The signposting along narrow roads, running between schist walls, will lead you through the village.

Follow the road towards the Loire (north-west). The GR3 takes the first path on the left immediately after the second bridge and, 200 metres further on, reaches an avenue lined with poplar trees. Turn left, cross a small bridge and turn right on to a path (shaded in summer) which passes close to the church of Juigné-sur-Loire.

The GR continues as far as the road; crosses it and carries on along a small path leading past slate walls and then across fields to the military road between Angers and Cholet. Turn left, go under the road and turn right for 100 metres. Turn left into a leisure park and follow the signposting. Turn left round the lake and, at the far end, walk north towards a path that leads to the D132; follow this road for 150 metres and then turn right on to a path running along an embankment by the Louet. This embankment leads via some steps to the N160, opposite a restaurant.

The GR3 turns left on to the N160 and follows it as far as Erigné.

Near the café-tabac, turn right down the road leading to the Louet, where it becomes a fishermen's path running along the foot of the cliff (Roche-de-Mûrs).

The GR3 leaves the Louet, goes round the

2Km
0:30

restaurant with a panoramic view and a monument commemorating the Wars of the Vendée. In 1793, the Vendean forces, led by Renée Bordereau, known as the Angevin, hurled 600 Republican soldiers from the top of the Roche-de-Mûrs into the Louet.

Varennes stadium and comes to the camp site at Mûrs-Erigné.

MÛRS – ERIGNÉ
Å ♨ 🚌

Aurignacian site at Grand-Claye; Roman camp at les Châtelliers; Château de la Moinerie (19th century) in the town of Mûrs; former Château de la Laudière (16th century); old houses at Gaigné and La Gillargière; Château des Châtelliers (19th century) at Garnier.

2Km
0:30

Head towards La Jubeaudière along a tarmac road; walk along the river to the village of Louet.

Louet

3Km
0:45

Near the transformer the GR3 turns left between two houses on to a path. At the Bois de Loup, it turns right and, on the bank of the Louet, left into an avenue lined with poplar trees which leeds to Le Pont-qui-Tremble.

Le Pont-qui-Tremble

The GR3 continues to follow the left bank of the Louet along D132.

Detour 15 mins
DENÉE
Å ♨ 🚌

Neolithic and Gallo-Roman settlements. Became a parish in 7th century, a fortified town in 12th century and has many 16th and 18th century houses. There are ruined windmills at les Grands Moulins and Puychartrain and a tower mill at Mantelon.

3Km
0:45

Leave the D132 to the right, opposite the Denée camp site, and cross a poplar plantation. As you leave the plantation, the path crosses a meadow (south) and crosses first a footbridge over a sluice gate and then, further on, a disused river channel. You will then come to Mantelon.

Mantelon

18th century château; 16th century turreted pavilion;

The GR3 goes up the road towards the N751 and after 400 metres, at the end of an estate, turns right into a wide path that passes the foot

The mills

From Montsoreau onwards, you cannot fail to notice the windmills, in various states of repair.

One hundred and fifty years ago, there were 640 windmills in Anjou. Today, the remains of 300 can still be seen and, thanks to the dynamic endeavours of the Association of the Friends of Windmills in Anjou and the assistance of the General Council of Maine-et-Loire, about 30 have been restored, eight of them to full working order. Three types of mill were used by millers in Anjou:

- Mills consisting of a cone of stone topped by a wooden cabin.
- Post mills, consisting simply of a large wooden frame to which the sails, transmission and millstones were attached.
- Tower mills, of which there are 167; 83 of them have retained their frame, and 21 their sails; two are still in operation.

3Km
0:45

19th century 'Thailand' pavilion; 18th century 'Logis Henri IV'; 19th century country houses.

La Garde
Panoramic views

2Km
0:30

ROCHEFORT-SUR-LOIRE
🏠 🛏 🍴 🚂 🚌
15th and 17th century houses in the town; ruined mills; 19th century church, 15th and 16th century belfry; chapel of Saint-Symphorien-en-Vallée; fountain and oratory of Saint-Lezin.

6Km
1:30

Detour *45 mins*
Béhuard
Place of pilgrimage for seafarers before 15th century; chapel built by Louis XI. Doll Museum. Take the D106 (north), take the bridge over the river and take the first turning on the right.

of the Moulin Neuf. After the mill, it turns left and then immediately right, following an indistinct path along a hedge bordering a field. After 100 metres, at the end of this field, you will pick up a good path leading to a minor road. Follow this road until you reach the N751, turn right and follow it for 50 metres, then turn left into the road to Les Loges. The GR goes through the hamlet and follows the road as far as Liaumerie. Cross the farmyard, and walk through the vineyards in a westerly direction until you will reach the old mill of La Garde.

After the mill, walk down the minor road and, shortly before La Poilanerie, turn left between a meadow and a vineyard and walk down into the wood. Caution Private property — do not stray from the signposted footpath. Cross a stream and walk to La Besnarderie. Follow the path on the right and then, 150 metres further on, turn left on to a path that follows the hillside as far as a tarmac road. Cross this road and enter a housing estate. The GR leaves the housing estate at the far end on the right-hand side and then follows a vineyard to reach Rochefort-sur-Loire.

The GR3 crosses the square behind the church and turns left up a street that narrows, turns right and leads to a road. Turn immediately left on to a path that will take you downhill across the stream of Saint-Lézin and then back uphill; after 1 kilometre you will come to a road. Turn right and then immediately left; follow another path along the edge of a small wood that will bring you to a track. The GR follows this track around the estate of L'Eperonnière. At the next bend, turn right on to another track that passes La Piécière. Before Le Raguenet, turn right and walk downhill as far as the N751. Turn left on to it; near Le Pressoir Girault, turn right on to a tarmac path along an arm of the Louet and walk up to La-Haie-Longue.

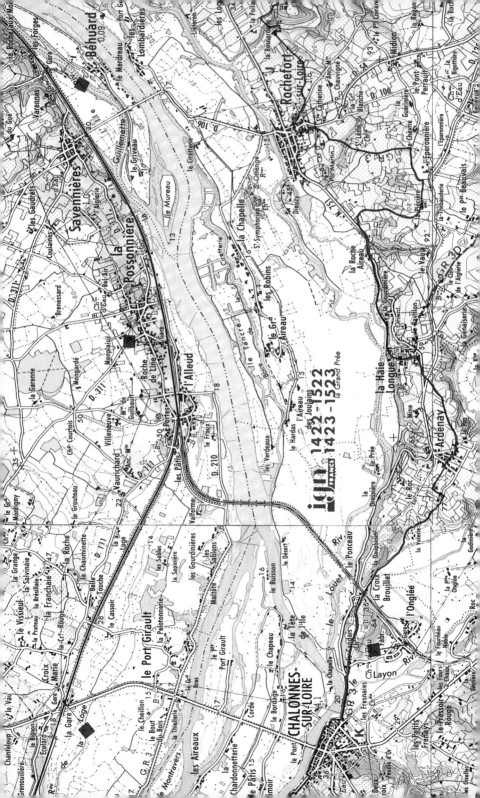

LA-HAIE-LONGUE
🍷 🚌

*Splendid view over the
meadows where the Angevin
aviator René Gasnier made
his first flights.
Chapel dedicated to Notre-
Dame-des-Aviateurs.*
**End of the alternative
route GR3D.**

2Km
0:30

ARDENAY
🍷 🚌

4Km
1

Detour *20 mins*
Chalonnes railway station
*Walk along the path on the
left that follows the railway
line. To continue see
page 136.*

The GR3 returns to the spot where it joined the
N751, but in order to avoid the heavy traffic
during the tourist season, goes past it and,
after the refreshment room, takes the second
road (signposted to the beach) going down
towards the Loire. Follow this road for 50
metres and turn left along a high wall bordering an estate. At the end of this wall, you will
rejoin the N751; follow it for 100 metres as far
as a small crossroads. Turn left; almost
immediately you will cross a minor road and
join a winding path that climbs through
vineyards to the hamlet of Ardenay.

Follow the GR signposting that will take you
through the alleyways to a path through the
vineyards. The footpath takes you behind the
mills (north) to a road. Follow it for 20 metres
and, where it turns sharply to the left (and
goes in front of the mills), turn off it and go
down a path (west) leading along the hillside.
You will go through the vineyards to a road
that skirts the vast meadows along the Layon.
This road goes uphill and then over a bridge
across the Angers-Cholet railway line.

The road continues to climb (panoramic views)
and then goes downhill again and joins N751
on a level with the Chalonnes camp site.

Chalonnes-sur-Loire
Situated at the confluence of the Loire and the Laon, 'Calonna', an ancient Druid
stronghold and then a Gallo-Roman settlement, was converted to Christianity in
the 5th century by Saint Maurille, a future bishop of Angers. Since that time, its
history has been inextricably linked with that of the bishopric. Sacked by the
Bretons and the Normans, the town experienced the vicissitudes of the Wars of
Religion and the Revolution (Wars of the Vendée). Chalonnes, which has been
a crossing place over the Loire since ancient times, has always been a
flourishing river port and commercial centre. It reached its zenith when the
Layon was canalized in the 18th century. In the 19th century, the coal mines
flourished, giving the town its modern appearance. Paleolithic settlement at Roc-
de-Pail.
On the island, remains of the apse of the chapel of the hermit Saint Hervé;
14th century Romanesque church of Sainte-Barbe-des-Mines currently being
restored; 15th century wayside shrine at La Bourgonnière.

The Layon Route

The alternative to GR3, known as the Layon route, begins 800 metres south-west of Trèves-Cunault and finishes at La Haie-Longue between Rochefort and Chalonnes-sur-Loire. It is 60 kilometres in length. There are two gîtes d'étapes offering overnight accommodation for walkers at Martigné-Briand and Beaulieu-sur-Layon; it is also possible to reserve accommodation at the Château de Launay at Louresse.

To start with, GR3D crosses a wooded region, then passes through troglodyte villages before joining the valley of the Layon, where it runs along the hills overlooking the river, sometimes following the old Petit Anjou railway line, which is now disused and has been made into a pleasant footpath.

This route turns away from the 'royal river' and its great châteaux to take the walker on a journey of discovery through the tranquil countryside of southern Anjou, with its villages and their small estates, its manor houses, old houses and windmills, and particularly its vineyards with their unchallenged reputation.

Trèves

7Km
1:15

Milly-le-Meugon

4.5km
1:10

The walk following the GR3D begins south-west of Trèves, on the Chemin de Saumur. GR3D follows a sunken path in a south-westerly direction; the path is in a bad state in winter and during bad weather. At a branching junction, 400 metres further on, take the path on the right through the wood. When you come out of the wood, turn left and skirt along the edge of it until you come to the D213 which finishes south of Maison Neuve.

Turn left and follow this road for 500 metres as far as a bend, then turn off to the right along a path through a wood. After 1.5 kilometres you will come out of the wood; turn left and you will come to a road where you turn right. Further on, 500 metres, turn left off it and turn immediately right and walk to Les Roches.

Before entering the hamlet, turn left on to a path along the wall surrounding Milly estate to the church and Château of Milly-le-Meugon.

Cross the D161, 150 metres further on, at the fork, continue straight on. After crossing one road you will come to the D69.

Turn left on to the D69 and follow it for 50 metres, then turn right on to a path that leads through undergrowth and vineyards for 3.5 kilometres to Villeneuve.

3.5Km
1

Villeneuve
The first troglodyte dwellings and barns can be seen in this hamlet.

6Km
1:30

Rochemenier
The troglodyte village and its museum of peasant life are worth visiting.

6Km
1:30

CHÂTEAU DE LAUNAY
Ⓗ

4Km
1

Brigné-sur-Layon
Small town in the middle of the vineyards that produce Rosé de Cabernet. 16th century priory. Château de Maurepart (15th-18th century) and Château de Boisairault. Group of mills known as the 'Three Bottles', and other ruined mills. 13th century church, restored in the 19th century; 18th century façade and panelling, 16th century stained-glass window.

MARTIGNÉ-BRIAND
△ ⚓

Parish in 12th century, chapter in 13th century. Old walled town. Menhir de la Grouas, also known as 'Gargantua's quoit'. Ruins of

Turn right, then, after 50 metres, turn left and go down a dirt track for 1.2 kilometres. Turn left to cross the road and, 400 metres further on, on the right, follow the path near the restored Moulin Gouré which has retained its gearing system. It leads to Rochemenier.

Follow the road to Doué-la-Fontaine and, as you leave the village, take the first path on the right. Follow it as far as the D761 (Angers-Poitiers), which you cross. The GR3d carries on along a secondary road opposite for 2 kilometres. When you come to the D159 turn left and follow it as far as the Château de Launay.

Walk to the D83 by turning right on leaving the estate and then immediately left. This road skirts the southern edge of the Launay estate. After about 1 kilometre, turn right on to a shell-marl path and, 500 metres further on, turn left and walk through the hamlet of La Basse-Banlée. Continue in a westerly direction to the D156: cross over and then turn left and walk along it for 50 metres. Turn right on to a path leading to Brigné-sur-Layon.

Walk west out of Brigné-sur-Layon; 200 metres from the crossroads, turn left on to a small path leading round La Croix Blanche, then turn left on to a broad path and follow it for one kilometre. Cross the road, skirt round Rouard wood, cross a stream and head towards Martigné-Briand, the chimneys of which are visible.

GR3D takes you through the town, crosses the D748 (Angers-Niort) and then enters an area of new housing. After the last house at the crossroads, follow the D125 in the direction of Thouarcé. A kilometre further on, leave the road and walk through the little wood (Bois des Brondes) along a path running parallel to the

9Km
2:15

16th century château: circular towers, stumps of chimneys. Château des Noyers (16th century), Château de Flines (18th century – 16th century fortified gateway). Four ruined windmills. Logis de la Tour, 15th-16th century, fortified gateway (farm). Church, 12th century and 19th century. Chapel of Soussigné: 15th century murals. 16th century chapel of Saint-Martin-des-Noyers (endangered masterpiece). Numerous wayside crosses, some of which date from the 15th and 16th centuries. Caution: For various reasons a provisional route has been laid out through Martigné-Briand, so follow the signposts carefully.

THOUARCÉ

Neolithic settlement. Parish before the 11th century. Walled town.

4Km
1

Church: 12th century belfry and portal, the rest is 19th century. 16th century stone virgin, 15th-18th century chalices. Two Romanesque chapels in the town. Iron-bearing springs at Les Grandes Fontaines.

FAYE D'ANJOU

Name is derived from the Latin word 'fagus', meaning 'beech'. Priory in 11th century. 15th century Château de Changé. Remains of the 16th century Château de Gilbourg. 18th century Logis de la Brunetière and 16th century

road. As you leave the wood, turn right on to a dirt track; walk past a pond and then turn left on to a path that leads to another one that follows a disused railway line. Turn right (northwest) and follow this path for about 2.5 kilometres through the midst of the vineyards until you reach a latticework fence. Bear right and walk uphill as far as La Croix de Fêle. Cross the D114 and follow a path that leads downhill towards a small wood. Turn left into this wood; when you come out of it, turn right on to the path along the old railway line (view over the valley of the Layon). After 1.5 kilometres you can turn off to the right and walk up to the Moulin de la Montagne. From here you will have panoramic views over the countryside.

The GR3D turns off to the left and leads downhill along a path; when you come to the D24, turn left and walk to Thouarcé.

Leave Thouarcé along the road to Faye d'Anjou; when you have left the town, turn right on to a small path leading back to the old railway line. Follow it for 1.7 kilometres as far as the D120. Turn right and follow it for 50 metres, then turn left on to a sunken path leading up the hill through broom and vines to the edge of Faye-d'Anjou.

Before the first houses of Faye d'Anjou, the GR turns left down the hill; it passes between the two mills of La Pinsonnerie and Guinechien. The path finishes below the old railway line: climb up to it and follow it for 500 metres to a clear space on the right; turn left on to a path winding along the side of the hill. Turn left and walk to a small wood and follow a pleasant path leading to the old railway line; turn right and follow the path to the D54.

Logis due Fresne. Château de Gastines, ruins of 15th century Château du Marchais. Several windmills, including la Pinsonnerie mill, complete with sails. The 12th century priory chapel (Chapelle du Lattay) is now a farm building. Neo-Gothic Chapelle du Sablon 1859.

8Km
2

Detour
Rablay-sur-Layon

Maple plantation mentioned in 11th century. Half-timbered house known as the 'tithe house' (post office). La Chauvellière and La Girardière 19th century châteaux. 18th century church. 18th century chapel in Mirebeau manor house. Turn left on to D54 and the Layon to Rablay.

Cross the D54 and, 600 metres further on, take a path parallel to the old railway line. About 450 metres further on, cross a road and walk up to Beaulieu-sur-Layon through the vines along a winding path that takes you past La Moulin du Roi.

BEAULIEU-SUR-LAYON

Dolmen de Mont-Benault. Hôtel Desmazières and Hôtel de la Pinsonnière – 18th century town houses. The town hall occupies a 16th century dwelling. Old mill (Moulin du Roy). 19th century church: 16th century Virgin and stall. Romanesque apse of the old church, converted into a chapel.

6.5Km
1:30

From the church, follow the road leading due west past a chapel, then turn left and, 40 metres further on, turn right. Follow this road, which becomes a path running alongside a small stream. Walk under the old railway line and continue along a path close to the river as far as the hamlet of Pont Barré.

Walk up to the N160 (formerly the N161 – Angers-Les-Sables-d'Olonne) and cross over. (The next section is a temporary route made necessary by the collapse of the hillside). Turn on to the tarmac path that leads to the D209; cross it and continue along a pleasant stretch of the river to Saint-Aubin-de-Luigné.

SAINT-AUBIN-DE-LUIGNÉ

16th century presbytery: gable window and mantlepiece bearing the coat of arms of Pope Alexander VI. Ruins of the Château de la Haute-Guerche: 13th century defensive walls, 15th

At the junction with the D106, along the continuation of the bridge over the Layon, between two houses, the GR heads north. About 600 metres further on, turn left and then follow a winding path up the hillside, passing close to Guérin mill.

La Grande-Brière

The marshes provided the inhabitants of la Grande-Brière with virtually all their resources. Hunting and fishing (with nets, with wicker pots and a sort of harpoon used for catching eels) were widely practised. Peat was used as fuel and was also sold in Nantes and throughout Brittany and Anjou. Mud from the ditches and dykes was used as fertilizer. Reeds are still used for thatched roofs, which are compulsory in some areas of the Park. They can also be put to other uses (notably pulp for paper making).

Many customs are associated with these activities, particularly in the communally-owned marshes. Many postcards from the early part of this century bear witness to the importance, at that time, of peat cutting, while at the same time revealing the successive stages of the process: the cutting of the blocks, the stacking into piles, often in such a way as to leave gaps to allow the peat to dry, and the transporting of the peat in 'cages', on carts, or punts, to the doors of the cottages.

Today he was going in a different direction — he started off along the sleeping furrows, lying immobile among the grass and weeds, across the disembowelled low-lying meadows, which always looked even more sunken under their black wounds. Green umbels lined his route. From time to time, a massive charred body raised the remains of unformed arms towards the sky; it was a fossilized tree, oak or beech, perhaps two thousand years old, extracted carefully from the peat bog, its heart blacker and harder than ebony. And everywhere the tall reeds billowed, providing shelter for wild birds. Now and then, he caught glimpses of pale stretches of water glistening through this jungle. Then islands of higher ground re-appeared, the reeds reformed and other stretches of water came into view; so it was that the Brière seemed endless, stretching as far as the last mists under the vast dome of the sky.

A. DE CHÂTEAUBRIANT

---

century towers, 14th century chapel, spherical oven. Château de la Fresnaye (16th century), Château de Paty (18th century), Château de la Genaiserie (18th century), Château de la Guerche (20th century). Manor houses in the village of La Haie-Longue. Church: 15th century tombstone, 16th century porch, 17th century reredos, 18th century terracotta Madonna.

4.5Km
1:15

La Haie-Longue

Continue north-west for 1.5 kilometres. Turn left on to the D125 and, after 200 metres, turn right on to a path leading uphill. Turn left 250 metres further on and walk to La Haie-Longue.

Here the GR3D meets the GR3.

CHALONNES-SUR-LOIRE

After crossing the Layon, the GR3 goes down towards the Loire and takes a path along it, between the river and the church. When you reach the embankment, go as far as the suspension bridge. Continue along the embankment, which, after a small square, narrows and becomes a towpath. Cross a small bridge with an iron parapet, turn left away from the Loire into a tunnel that passes under the ruins of the château and the N751. You will come out at the Rue du Château; turn right (west) on to it and, after 200 metres, you will come to a small square. Instead of turning right, continue straight on along a narrow road (Rue de la Tannerie) leading to the N751. Cross this road and go down the Rue de l'Enfer to the Loire. Follow the path for a few hundred metres and then, on a level with an old lime kiln, bear left

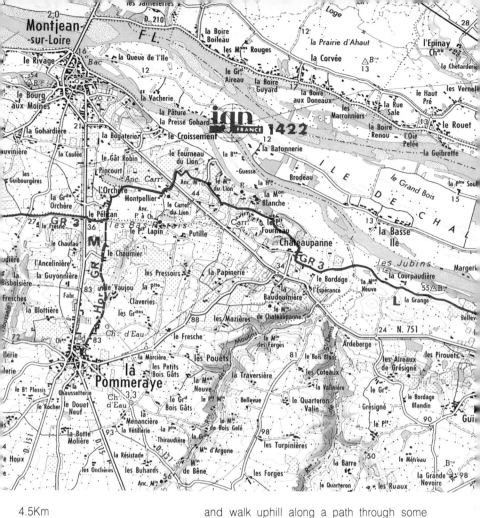

4.5Km
1:15

and walk uphill along a path through some copses. This path will bring you to a minor road (dead-end) that you will follow for about 1 kilometre.

Before Bellevue farm, you will see an isolated house on the right; take the grassy path leading round this house and down to the Loire. At the first turning (200 metres), leave this path and turn left (west) across a meadow; you will pick up a path through the woods, running parallel to the Loire and overlooking it for a stretch of about 40 metres. Shortly afterwards, the GR3 enters the meadow and skirts the wood as far as the cemetery.

Caution The cemetery is private property, but thanks to the owner's generosity you are allowed to cross it; please keep to the signposted path.

The path now goes downhill, skirting a dense hedge on the right (the river side). At the bottom of the hill, cross a fence close to a crossroads.

Carrefour des Jubins

Follow the path leading in a westerly direction across a small bridge (Pont des Jubins) and through Les Rosiers to the hamlet of Château-panne.

Châteaupanne
Former church, now a barn, of the 10th, 12th and 15th centuries; remains of 12th-century fresco.

As soon as you reach the first houses, turn right (north-east) around the priory and continue along the minor road for a further 100 metres. At a sharp left-hand bend in sight of a small bridge, the GR turns off this road and follows a path on the left, bordered by a wall, that will take you up along the top of some old quarries. This path becomes a road and passes La Maison Blanche. After the entrance to this property (two large pilllars), bear slightly right and follow the road between two windmills that have lost their sails. At the second mill, take the small path on the left which, after 300 metres (small square house), divides into two at the tarmac track on the left (south-west); after a few minutes, you will come to the junction with the N751.

3.5Km
1

CD 751
Detour *20 mins*
MONTJEAN-SUR-LOIRE
🏠 ⛺ ✕ 🚉 🚌
Primitive settlement; 10th century stronghold with fortified château; 13th century granite cross in cemetery; ruins of the 13th century chapel of Saint-Jean de-l'Aumonerie; 19th century church with 16th century pietà and 18th century fonts. 19th century Oratory of Saint-Méen; ruins of lime kilns.

Detour see left. To go to Montjean − the church steeple is clearly visible from the GR − follow either N751 or minor roads running parallel to it in a north-westerly direction.

The GR3 crosses the N751 and follows a road directly opposite which turns right and then left. At this last bend, turn off the road on to a path that leads in a westerly direction to a former quarry filled with water. Here, bear south: the path will join a road that will bring you to Les Bas-Retais.

5Km
1:15

139

Le Bas-Retais
Detour *20 mins*
LA POMMERAYE
🏠 🏕 ⚒

*Paleolithic settlements;
parish in the 11th century;
18th century windmill at la
Roche-Evière, now restored;
ruined windmill; 19th century
church; ruins of the 15th
century Chapelle des
Forges; ruins of 17th century
chateau at Putille.
Continue straight on (south).*

From Le Bas-Retais, the GR3 turns right (west) along a tarmac road. It crosses the D151, passes through L'Arche Longue, Les Cailleries and Les Préaux and comes to Le Pressoir.

Le Pressoir

3Km
0:45

At the crossroads, bear left, then turn left again to walk uphill along the edge of a wood; you will come to a road. Bear right (west). Cross the millstream at the Benois mill and, 200 metres further on, turn left on to a path that leads up towards le Haut Puiset. At the end of this path at the gate, turn right; walk along the farm buildings and then go down to the road along a tree-lined path. At a crossroads, bear left and then turn immediately right on to a tarmac path that leads across a small bridge to the entrance of the 19th century Château du Vaugirault. From here, a dirt track leading up along the edge of the estate will bring you to Le Mesnil-en-Vallée.

LE MESNIL-EN-VALLÉE

19th century church; 18th century cemetery chapel.

2.5Km
0:40

The GR3 follows the D150 as far as a small, tree-lined square and goes across it in a westerly direction towards the Pinot mill, leaving the Buttes and Vent mills on the left. At the crossroads before the Pinot mill, ignore the roads on the right and left, and follow a path that starts in the field opposite; it is barely visible to start with, but it quickly becomes a good footpath that will take you down through woods to the ruins of Sour mill. Turn right on to the path that bears left 200 metres further on and then leads uphill in a southerly direction. At the top of the hill, enter a meadow on the right and walk to D222. Follow this road in a southerly direction to Saint-Laurent-du-Mottay.

SAINT-LAURENT-DU-MOTTAY

Château de la Houssaye (19th century); 15th century Croix de la Barre; 17th century Virgin.

2.5Km
0:35

The GR3 follows the D222 (south-west) out of the town and at the last houses, on a sharp bend, takes a sunken road opposite that leads downhill to L'Etang. Turn right on to a path along the pond that finishes 500 metres further on at a stream. Turn left. After a further 200 metres, you will come to a second pond. Take the right fork and walk uphill as far as La Réholière. Here, follow the road for 200 metres, then turn off at a sharp bend along a path bordered by hedges. After a further 300 metres, turn left on to a path that passes close to the tower of an old mill; turn left down the path leading to La Marcheboire farm.

La Marcheboire

Leave the farm to the right (north-west) along a good path that gradually disappears along the edge of the fields. You will then come to a tree-

lined path that goes downhill to a minor road, meeting it virtually opposite Bizerie farm. Turn left and follow the road for 1 kilometre.

On this section of the GR, it has not been possible to avoid tarmac roads, but the route does take you along farm service roads where there is very little traffic.

The GR3 turns right and passes la Grande Vacherie. The road goes downhill for quite a long way and joins the N751.

N751

4Km
1

Turn right on to this road and follow it for about 400 metres (on the river side, a small footpath has been cut into the bank). Turn left. Walk along a tarmac road across a stream to a vast area of meadows; the GR goes across these meadows, firstly north, then west. After 2 kilometres you will come to the causeway; follow it in a westerly direction as far as Le Pont de Vallée. Cross the bridge and follow the fisherman's path firstly along the arm of the Loire and then through some gardens. After 800 metres, you will come to the quays of Saint-Florent-le-Vieil.

SAINT-FLORENT-LE-VIEIL

ⓗ △ ⚠ ✕ ⇆ ⇆

Gallo-Roman settlement at Mont Glonne. Hermitage of Saint Florent in 4th century. Religious community established on site of his tomb was reorganized in 7th century by Saint Mauron. Expelled by the Normans, the monks fled to Tournus in 9th century, taking relics of Saint Florent with them. 11th century Danish encampment and port on L'Ile Batailleuse. Walled town. Scene of 1793 insurrection in the War of the Vendée. Remains of old Norman port on river bed. The town is perched on a hill overlooking the Loire. Former Benedictine abbey (17th century). Streets lined with old houses. Former Chapel of the Sacred Heart

2Km
0:30

Alternative route if you are experiencing wet weather. Cross the Loire and take a short-distance footpath to Oudon which avoids the route through Champtoceaux which can be hazardous if the going is wet. The views are less beautiful than those on the GR route; the footpath is marked by purple signposts.

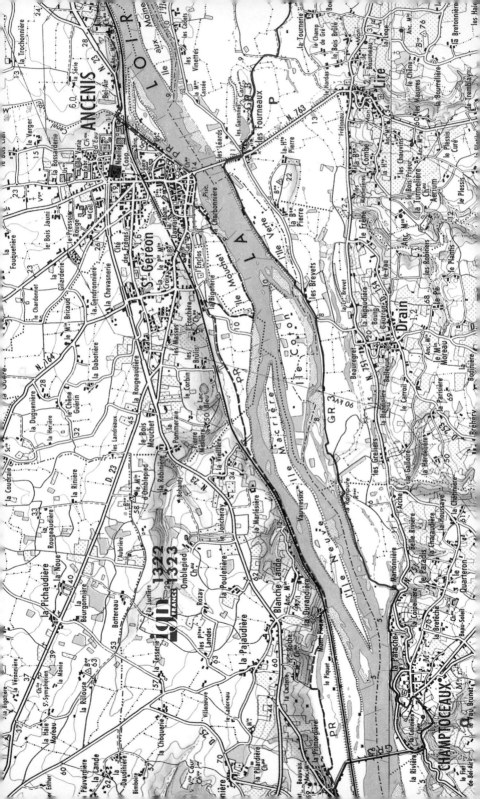

Saint-Florent-le-Vieil

Walkers may spend the night at the ferme des Coteaux (the farm, where there is an aquarium containing fish from the Loire, is currently being restored). At the beginning of the 4th century, Florent founded a monastery at Mont-Glonne. Having come to the foot of a grotto hollowed out of the cliff overlooking the Loire, Florent expelled the snakes who inhabited it. Having thus purified the grotto, he installed himself in it in order to thank the Lord. He built an oratory and inspired miracles. Saint-Florent died on the 22nd of September at the age, so it is said of 123. The successor to Saint-Florent, Saint-Mauron, rid the villages of a monstrous snake by killing it. This dragon would leap on his victims, pierce them a thousand times with his forked tongue, cover them with a ghastly foam and crush their bones before eating them with great relish. Saint-Mauron is reputed to have slept for 100 years.

is now a museum of local history.

The GR3 passes under the arch of the bridge and continues along the left bank of the Loire for 1.5 kilometres. Shortly before the confluence of the Evre and the Loire, it climbs up through gardens and poplar plantations towards Notre-Dame-du-Marillais.

Notre-Dame-du-Marillais
Sactuary, place of pilgrimage.

5Km
1:15

Without going as far as the road and the bridge, go west down a small, steep path that will take you across a ford downstream of the bridge. Continue straight on for 200 metres and then turn right on to a path that will take you to the bank of the Loire and then across meadows and poplar plantations. It turns sharply away from the Loire and then forks to the left in the direction of La Loge-de-Vallée.

LA LOGE-DE-VALLÉE
Λ ℽ

2.5Km
0:35

From here, turn right and walk west for 150 metres, then turn left (south) on to a road leading to a crossroads. Here, turn right on to a wide path which, 1 kilometre further on, joins a road (statue of Notre-Dame-de-la-Vallée). Turn left and follow the road south for 500 metres; turn right on to a broad path that will take you round the hamlet of Le Fossé Neuf.

Le Fossé Neuf
Detour *15 mins*
LA GUICHETIÈRE
⌂

5Km
1:15

The GR3 turns left and leads uphill in a south-westerly direction. Follow a road that passes close to an old quarry on the left, which is now flooded. After this quarry, turn right onto a tarmac path that passes through La Vasinière. A further 600 metres on turn left (west) and walk along wide avenues, bordered by poplars, past some former quarries, now flooded,

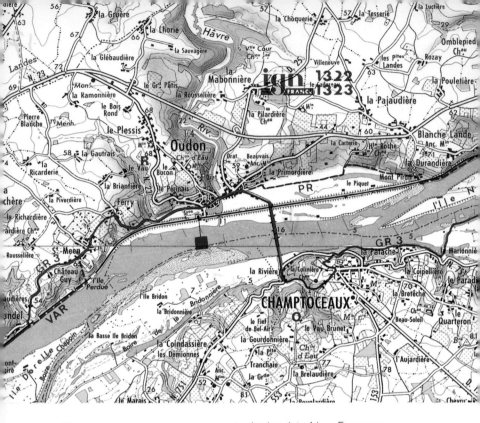

to the hamlet of Les Fourneaux.

Les Fourneaux
Detour *20 mins*
LIRÉ
🏠 ✕ 🚌

*Ruins of former château de
la Turmelière (15th century).
Modern château de la
Turmelière (sanatorium) 19th
century, neo-Louis XIII.
Château de la Beuvrie, de la
Plissonnière et du Chêne.
Four windmills and two water
mills in ruins. 19th century
church. Chapelle de
Beaulieu 1771.
Follow the N763 to the
south.*

2.5Km
0:40

The GR3 turns right on to the N763 towards
Ancenis.

Detour *10 mins*
ANCENIS
🏠 ✕ 🚉 🚌

Continue north over the

The GR3 turns off the road before the bridge
and follows a path going down towards the
bank of the Loire. It crosses a sandpit and,
800 metres further on, the path forks to the

bridge. *A short-distance footpath leads directly to Oudon along the right bank of the Loire (10 kilometres).*

Les Brevets

4.5Km
1:30

La Patache

2.5Km
0:40

right, leads round a farm and peters out. It then becomes a fisherman's path skirting the meadows along the Loire. In a distance of 1.5 kilometres, you will come to a series of fences which can be crossed by means of small zigzag passages. The GR joins the road at Les Brevets.

Follow this road for about 500 metres and, as it turns left, leave it and continue straight on along a sandy path skirting. water holes. Further on, after 2 kilometres, you will come to a path on the left lined with poplars. Ignore this and, 300 metres further on, you will come to La Rompure, a tumbledown house on the right. On the downstream side of the ruins, walk through the meadow along a path that follows the hedge to the bank of the Loire, then walk due north along a pasture and you will come to a small embankment on the edge of the river. Follow this embankment for 1.5 kilometres and then turn off it to the left. Cross the footbridge over a sluice gate and enter a meadow. Cross the meadow in a south-westerly direction along a small depression. The GR goes alongside an old overgrown path. At the far end of the meadow, go through a gate and walk along a tree-lined path running along the top of a small stone embankment. At the end of this embankment, shortly after crossing another footbridge over a sluice gate, and in sight of an overgrown cliff, turn right and go down into a sandy, grassy area along an arm of the Loire, which may be dry or damp underfoot, depending on the time of year. You will come to an area of rocks overhanging this arm of the river.

Caution Cross this area with caution, since it may be dangerous in rainy weather.

The GR3 joins a footpath that takes you to La Patache.

Walk west through the hamlet and, at a bend in the road leading to the N751, take a path between the Loire on the right and a cliff on the left. After a steep uphill section, 1 kilometre further on, cross the N751 and take a path virtually opposite up to Champtoceaux.

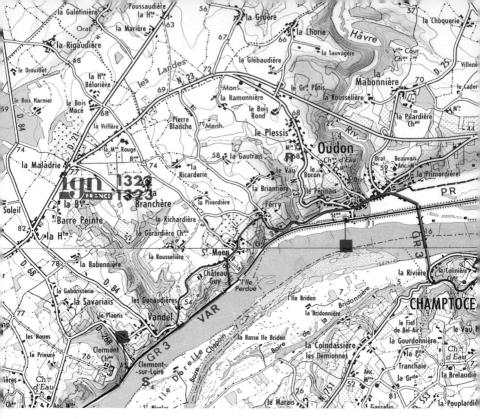

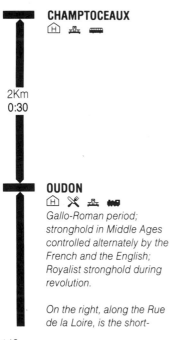

CHAMPTOCEAUX

🏠 � ▭

2Km
0:30

OUDON

🏠 🍴 🚢 🛥

Gallo-Roman period;
stronghold in Middle Ages
controlled alternately by the
French and the English;
Royalist stronghold during
revolution.

On the right, along the Rue
de la Loire, is the short-

When the GR3 reaches the square near the entrance to the château (panoramic view 300 metres on the left), it takes the first street on the right and, 200 metres further on, turns right on to a tree-lined path that leads down to the bottom of a valley. The path first bears right and then sweeps round to the left 600 metres further on and joins the N751. Turn right and follow this road as far as a new bridge, then cross the Loire. Having crossed the Loire and thë the railway, continue straight on as far as the outskirts of Oudon.

Champtoceaux
Celtic settlement. Gallo-Roman port and stronghold overlooking the Loire on an exceptional site on the border between Anjou and Brittany. Castrum Sellis (high castle) was one of the 25 principal Roman camps in Gaul. Parish in the sixth century. Residence of Pépin le Bref who, in 768, received the ambassadors of the Caliph of Baghdad there. Subject of many conflicts between the dukes of Brittany and the counts of Anjou. Besieged and destroyed by Saint-Louis in 1230. Priory in the 11th century. Walled town torn down in the 15th century and then reconstructed. Devastated by the 'infernal columns' in 1794. Remains of 11th century defensive wall. Former presbytery (18th century). Ruins of feudal château destroyed in the 14th century: 'Devil's Tower'. Fortified toll point on the Loire (12th century). Former Château de la Hamelière (17th century): moats, towers. New château built in the 19th century in a neo-Louis XIII style. Former Châteaux de la Colinière and de la Bretèche (19th century). Ruined windmills. Former Château de la Brelaudière 16th century, burnt down in 1793 (farm). In the 19th century church: 14th century processional cross and 17th century Virgin painted on wood.
  Panoramic view from the Promenade du Champalud, 90 metres above the valley of the Loire. There is a park surrounding the ruins of the château.

distance footpath marked by purple signposts from Saint-Florent-le-Vieil.

Just before the church, turn left along Rue Alphonse-Fouschard.

Just before the Hâvre, on the right, there is a short-distance footpath signposted in yellow and white. There are footpaths, maintained by the local authorities, along both banks of the Hâvre.

Warning on the footpath itineraries displayed in the town, the route indicated for the GR is not the same as that authorized by the FFRP-CNSGR.

2.5Km
0:45

Walk past the foot of the tower which was formerly the castle keep. In front of the Hôtel-restaurant du Port the GR3 turns left (Place du Port) and then immediately right, going along the road out of Oudon. It soon starts to climb up the hillside overlooking the valley of the Loire. As you enter Ferry, turn left on to a path which, shortly afterwards, leads into the vineyard: continue straight on. On your left and behind you, immense panorama over the Loire and Oudon. At Saint-Méen, you will come to a minor road: carry straight on. As you leave Saint-Méen you will come to the alternative route.

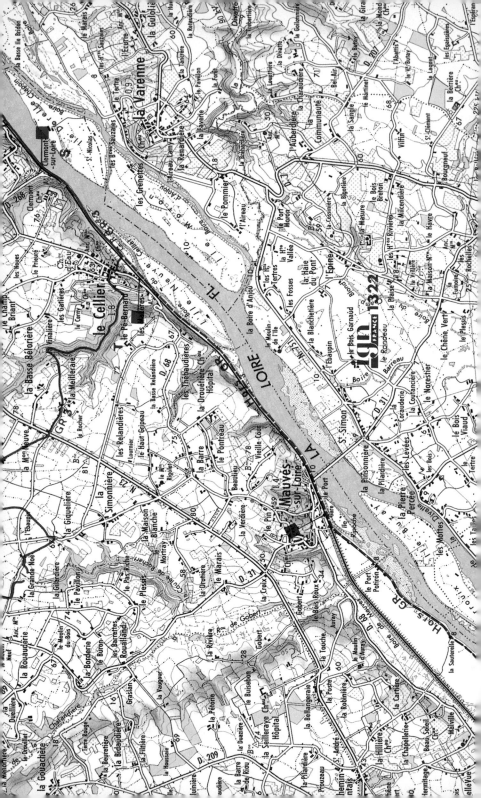

Grapes, wine and winemakers

There are 25,000 hectares of vineyards in Anjou, producing rosé (45 per cent), white (30 per cent) and red wines (25 per cent). There are three rosés: rosé de Loire, which is exclusively dry; rosé d'Anjou, medium-dry, and Cabernet d'Anjou, invented by M. Taveau in 1905. Rosé is a delicate fruity wine, with a beautiful purplish pink colour and a raspberry bouquet; in the Saumurois, it is full-bodied with an added note of elegance and lightness.

There are also three types of white wine: the medium-dry, made from the white Chenin grape, must be served chilled and, if possible, after it has matured in the bottle for several years. The dry white, made from the white Chenin grape, possibly blended with Chardonnay, is a firm, thoroughbred wine, which is both delicate and fruity. In the Saumurois, it is more strongly characterized by the limestone (tufa) on which the grapes are grown. The Coteau de Layon produces a great sweet white wine, with a magnificent golden colour with green highlights. Its delicate bouquet is captured as early as the spring following the harvest, but it takes several years for the wine to mature.

The winemaker of the Anjou is the son of Rabelais.

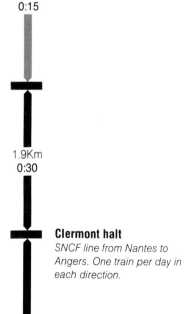

Junction

1.1Km
0:15

1.9Km
0:30

Clermont halt
SNCF line from Nantes to Angers. One train per day in each direction.

Alternative route Follow the path on the left along the wall of the Château de Saint-Méen. A little further on it goes down towards the Loire. The paths on the right will take you, in five minutes, to the ruins of the Folies-Siffait, a promontory site with fine views over the Loire. Pass under the railway between two tunnels and join the towpath. Turn right on to it, alongside the railway lines. After the second railway tunnel you will rejoin the GR3 footpath.

The GR3 continues along the road that follows the top of the hill and goes through the vineyard. On the other bank, on top of the wooded slope, you can see the Château de Varenne. The road comes to an end at Les Génaudières. Continue straight on along the path as it leads down into the valley. After passing under the railway line, you will come to the towpath and the link with the alternative route. Turn right on to the towpath.

Continue along the towpath which leads round the Clermont railway tunnel under the grounds of the Château de Clermont, and, immediately afterwards, passes the 'Beau Rivage' bar-restaurant. After 100 metres the road that leaves from the restaurant turns and goes underneath the railway line. Continue straight on along the towpath for 1.7 kilometres until

you reach the second pedestrian subway under the railway.

Detour see left. A very pleasant route (which it is planned to use for a long-distance footpath through the basin of the Sèvre and Loire) will take you to Nantes. All you have to do is to continue straight on without going under the railway line. You will pass through the various places listed left.

Detour
NANTES via:
15 min
Cellier Halt
Nantes-Angers line. One train per day in either direction.

1.9Km
0:30   *1 hr*
Mauves-sur-Loire
Nantes-Angers line. Several trains each day.

2 hr 20 mins
Thouaré
Nantes-Angers line. TAN bus services, route 92, to Nantes. Voulon town hall. Tramway connection to city centre.

3 hr 30 mins
Bellevue
TAN bus services, route 83, to Nantes, Haluchère. Tramway connection to city centre.

4 hr 20 mins
Nantes
(Malakoff district). TAN bus service, line 56, serving the city centre.

LE CELLIER
🏠 ✕ ⟡ ⚓ 🚌 ▭
Network of short-distance

the GR3 turns right under the railway line and up a good, fairly steep path (chemin de Sault) to Le Cellier.

The GR3 turns right into the Rue des Mazères and then immediately left into the Rue Notre-Dame. At the end of this road, take the path

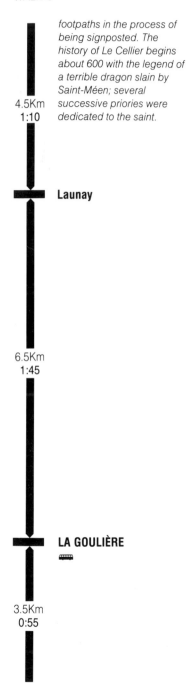

footpaths in the process of being signposted. The history of Le Cellier begins about 600 with the legend of a terrible dragon slain by Saint-Méen; several successive priories were dedicated to the saint.

4.5Km
1:10

Launay

6.5Km
1:45

LA GOULIÈRE

3.5Km
0:55

opposite leading sharply downhill. You will come to a small stream; follow the path leading upstream along the water, crossing over twice and ignoring several paths leading to the plateaux on either side. At La Croix-des-Renards, the confluence of two streams, follow the right-hand one (north, then north-west). Keeping to the bottom of the valley, you will cross a new road and walk through a tunnel under the N23; following a recently cleared path, the GR3 crosses the stream several times and comes to Launay.

Turn left on to the road leading to the pond. As you leave the hamlet, turn right on to a wide path linking plots of agricultural land. At the end of the path, take another one on the left, which soon becomes lined with hedges. Cross a road and take another path virtually opposite (slightly to the right). At the end of this path, follow the road on the left and almost immediately, before the first house in La Gicquelière, take a path on the right as far as La Noë Source. Turn left on to the road, walk under the motorway and, at the first crossroads, turn right towards Long-Champ. Continue straight on for a little over a kilometre and then, just before a road, turn left on to a path. At the next crossroads, turn right on to the D31; at the next crossroads, bear left on to a tarmac path that leads to a farm, turns left and then right, crosses the railway line and bears left. Turn sharply right off this path on to a partly-hidden grassy path running along the edge of a meadow. At the end of this path, turn left along a row of trees, leave the meadow through the gap in the fence and continue along the path. Turn right on to the D9 to reach La Goulière.

Turn left, then at the next crossroads turn left again. The road bears right, follow it, and then carry straight on, sometimes on a road, sometimes on a path, for more than 2 kilometres, passing through La Davièrerie. From here, you overlook the basin of the Erdre opposite (plain of Mazerolles and marsh of Saint-Mars). At the end of the road, turn right then left at the next crossroads, right again and then left on to a path which takes you to the N178 at La Banque.

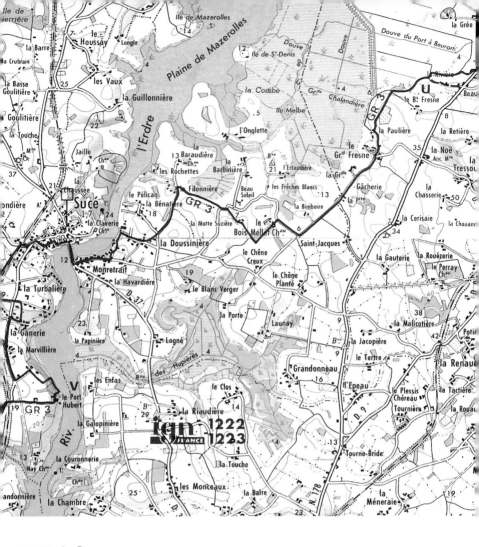

La Banque
Detour *15 mins*
BEAUCHÊNE

Detour see left. From this crossroads, follow a minor road on the left for 200 metres to the hamlet of Beauchêne. In the reverse direction, from the bus stop, follow the signs to the river ('la Rivière'). You will pick up the GR3 at the first crossroads, as it approaches from the right and carries on to the left.

The GR crosses the N178 (be careful) and follows a path opposite that skirts a farm, turns left, then right and at the next crossroads carries straight on. It skirts the marsh of Saint-Mars and then starts to lead uphill. It turns left towards la Pauliere along a wide tarmac path,

leading to the top of the rise, from where you can see the entire marshes of Saint-Mers and the valley of the Erdre.

The path leads down on the opposite site of the hill, passes La Paulière, turns left and becomes a minor road. At Le Grand Fresne cross a road and continue straight on for 1.3 kilometres. Pass through La Petite Gâcherie, leaving the road leading to La Bimboire on your right, and take the first minor road to the right; a little further on, at the turning, take the left-hand path.

Caution You are now entering private property; the owner has kindly agreed to allow walkers to cross his land; please do not wander from the GR.

Walk past the Château du Bois Mellet; cross the main avenue leading up to it and continue straight on along a path skirting meadows and woods; at the end of this path, turn right. At La Motte Suzière farm carry on along the minor road opposite and, at the first crossroads, turn left and almost immediately, at the turning, take the path leading off to the right. You will come to a minor road leading from the Château de la Baraudière, which is visible on the right-hand side; turn left on to it.

When you reach Les Roches Blanches, leave the road to Le Pélican and La Bénatière on your right and, immediately afterwards, bear right on to a small, unmade road. When you reach another road, turn right on to it; at the next crossroads, where there is an old baker's oven, continue straight on. You will soon come to a public beach on the banks of the Erdre; turn left and, at the end of the promenade, turn left again along a footpath (Ruelle Tassin) bordered by several residential properties, beyond which the Erdre can be glimpsed. Turn right on to the road leading down to the river. Turn right at the bottom, cross the bridge and, immediately afterwards, follow the steps on the left down to the lower embankment. You are now in the centre of Sucé.

**8.5Km
2:10**

SUCÉ-SUR-ERDRE
🏠 ⛺ ✕ 🍷 🚊 🚌

There was a Roman town on this site, and it owes its name to its many fig trees, the Latin for which is sulcus. *Before the revoking of the Edict of Nantes, Sucé was an active centre of Protestantism. Descartes, whose family owned two manor houses here, often came to the banks of the Erdre. During the Revolution, the town was a refuge for rebellious priests, but during*

The GR3 follows the Erdre downstream to the end of the quay. It turns right along the Rue du Port, then left (Rue du Pin) and right (still the Rue du Pin), crosses the D69 and bears left on to the D49 (Rue de Treillières). Cross the railway line and turn immediately left (Rue des Mésanges); this road becomes a grassy path that goes downhill below the level of the railway line. Continue straight on along the SNCF line, from which the path does not stray until the end, where it turns to go round a house. When you come to a minor road turn left on to it, walk over the level crossing, cross the D69 and take the first road on the right which soon becomes a path; cross a minor road and continue straight on. You will come to the D69; turn left and follow it for 800 metres.

the Terror particularly bloody retribution was exacted.

Caution: dangerous turning.

After La Marvillière, leave the D69 and turn left, then right. When the path bears left to enter a private estate, continue straight on along the edge of a meadow. The path is barely visible any longer, since it is overgrown with grass and hidden under the branches of trees. It improves beyond the meadow and comes to an end at a fence. From here, the GR goes across a series of three private estates, including that of the Port Hubert. Permission has been given for the GR to cross this private land. Make sure you close the gates, and follow the signposts to the Erdre; otherwise,

7Km
1:45

you may walk anywhere provided there are no signs saying 'Private' ('Privé'). Turn left between the hedge and the barbed wire fence, cross two fences and enter the wood. Shortly afterwards, you will walk down a very steep slope to the bank of the Erdre; turn right and walk along the river for 150 metres.

At this point a stroll along the Erdre beyond the GR3, as far as the edge of the Port Hubert estate is highly recommended.

The GR goes up on the right-hand side back into the wood and bears immediately left. Cross the small car park for the estate and turn right. You will come to the D69; turn left and follow it for 1 kilometre, walking underneath the railway line and above Le Boire-de-Nay.

Caution This section of the road, which includes two blind bends, is dangerous; wherever possible, walk behind the safety barrier. Traffic is soon to be diverted, which should ensure greater safety for walkers.

Immediately after crossing the Boire-de-Nay, turn right towards La Charlière; a little further on turn left towards La Hergrenière and walk past Le Tertre.

The Erdre

The Erdre, in the view of the people of the Nantais, is the most beautiful river in France. Bordered sometimes by wooded slopes, and sometimes by marshlands, the stretch of the river followed by the GR3 reaches a maximum width of 900 metres, forming a series of magnificent stretches of smooth water much frequented, at weekends, by large crowds of people sailing and rowing. The unusual width of this stretch of the river is due, in part, to a rise in the level of the sea but the Erdre was widened still further when its course was dammed at Nantes during the construction of the Nantes-Brest canal, of which it constitutes the first section. The conditions under which this operation was carried out (without expropriation or compensation) means that there are no rights of way; nevertheless, the local authorities in the Nantes area are gradually negotiating such rights, which will make it possible to establish short-distance footpaths. The Erdre is lined by an impressive series of châteaux (12 in as many kilometres between Nantes and Sucé-sur-Erdre); most were built in the 17th and 18th centuries by wealthy citizens of Nantes, shipowners and industrialists who came to spend their summers on the banks of the river. At that time, Nantes was a very prosperous city, the largest port in Europe.

At this point, the GR is joined from the right by one of the walks in the network of short-distance footpaths around La Chapelle-sur-Erdre. Known as the 'circuit du Rup', it is signposted in blue-and-white and follows the same route as GR3 until it leaves La Chapelle-sur-Erdre.

The GR3 follows a road that becomes a path leading down towards the Rupt. It crosses this at the far end of a small pond and leads back up the opposite slope. Just before La Chapelle-sur-Erdre, it turns right on to the old railway line.

LA CHAPELLE-SUR-ERDRE
Å ✗ ℩ ☐ ☐ ☐
Detour
7.3Km
Nantes (La Jonelière)
TAN bus service, route 51 for city centre.
NANTES (LE PETIT PORT)
Å ✗ ℩

Detour see left. A route signposted in green and white leads from the Place de l'Eglise. This detour will take you to some highly recommended beautiful sites along the Erdre, which are not accessible by car. It is possible to return to La Chapelle-sur-Erdre by TAN buses, nos. 86, 25 or 96, or on foot: a little before La Jonelière another footpath, also signposted in green and white, leads back to the starting point via the Château de l'Hopitau and the valley of the Gesvres, completing a round trip of 15 kilometres.

Continue along the old railway line until it crosses a road. A 30-kilometre section of this railway line, which went to Blain, has been purchased in order to create a track for walking and horse riding.

When the GR reaches a road, turn left.

La Chapelle-sur-Erdre
There was a Neolithic settlement on the site, but little is known of its ancient history. From the 13th century onwards, the history of La Chapelle-sur-Erdre merges with that of the Château de la Gâcherie. Having succeeded the de Lespervier family, the La Noue family, who were Calvinists, made welcome many Protestants from Nantes; then the de Charette family remained until the Revolution, during which the inhabitants of La Chapelle took the side of the Chouans and always succeeded in driving out the conforming priests imposed upon them. Many other châteaux, built in the 17th and 18th centuries, are scattered throughout the area, particularly along the banks of the Erdre. La Chapelle-sur-Erdre is still an important agricultural town, but increasingly it is becoming a residential suburb of Nantes.

Opposite and to the right is the beginning of two branches of the short-distance footpath.

You will cross another road almost immediately; continue straight on along the Rue de la Bussonnière. On the edge of La Bussonnière, bear left on to a path leading alongside a farm. It very quickly meets a path; turn left on to it, and leave it at the first bend along a path leading down to the right. You will come to a road leading to L'Evandière farm. Follow this road; at the end, turn right, follow the road as far as the Massigné bridge over the Gesvres.

At this point, you can pick up the 'Chemin des Vallées', a short-distance footpath

Just before the bridge, turn left on to the path along the Gesvres, which is a tributary of the Erdre. Shortly before the Forge bridge, walk uphill to the left along a path and turn right at

7.2Km
1:50

signposted in yellow and black.

The short-distance footpath mentioned above starts on the left.

On the right is the starting point for another section of the 'Chemin des Vallées', signposted this time in green and white. You can follow this route to the Verrière aqueduct and the Château de l'Hôpitau. Continue along the Erdre and then take a magnificent route, also signposted in green and white and often following the bank of the river, turning right towards Nantes or left to La Chapelle-sur-Erdre.

On the right is the starting point for another footpath along the other bank of the Gesvres which joins the previous one at the Verrière viaduct; it is passable only in dry weather.

LE TÉLÉGRAPHE

the top of the hill.

You will come to a road; turn right on to it and then immediately afterwards, at the 'Stop' sign, turn right again.

Cross the Gesvres by the Forges bridge.

A little further upstream, on the bend, take the road on the right and cross the stream known as Le Douet de la Bitaudais.

Caution: the route may be subject to change in order to avoid the road. Follow the signposts carefully.

In the hamlet of La Gergaudière, turn left at the crossroads and, 30 metres further on, bear right on to a broad path that leads past three houses, and then narrows and continues between two hedges. When you come to a minor road, turn right. At the hamlet of La Cathelinière, this road turns left and then bears slightly right; at the second bend, bear left on to a path. The path broadens and joins a road. Turn left and, 500 metres further on, you will come to the N137 at Le Télégraphe.

Cross the N137 by a bridge over an express way. Immediately afterwards turn right along a minor road and follow it for 300 metres. When you come to another road, turn left and walk to La Barre farm. The road becomes a grassy track leading to the Petit Moulin de la Tour. On a level with the farm, turn right along a path

leading through a wood. At the end of this path you will come to the Château de la Tour. Turn left round the château and start walking along a wide, straight avenue.

3.2Km
0:50

The path coming from the right is a short-distance footpath of 4.5 kilometres, signposted in green, which follows the same route as the GR3 as far as Orvault.

This avenue becomes a path leading to Le Plessis Buron. The GR goes past the houses, turns left on to a road which crosses a small stream and leads up through a small wood. Turn right on to a path near the entrance to an estate; this leads to a minor road where you turn right. You will come to the Château du Loret (one of 23 in the Orvault district!), skirt round a stretch of water and come to the D75.

On the right is the junction with another branch of the short-distance footpath, signposted in green, which, 150 metres further on, turns left on to the D42.

The D75 will take you into the town of Orvault.

ORVAULT
🏠 🗻 🍴 🍷 ⚓ 🚂

The old town, has retained much of its original character. There was a settlement on the site as early as the Gallo-Roman period, and many remains have been found.

Detour *1-2 hr*
Pont du Cens

Detour see left. A very pleasant route, signposted in light blue, will take you down the valley of the Cens to Pont du Cens.

This route can be extended by 4 kilometres towards the confluence of the Erdre and the Cens. Junction with the path leading to La Chapelle-sur-Erdre. Nantes Youth Hostel, near the SNCF station.

From the town centre, a short-distance footpath (3 kilometres) signposted in light green. Other walks, signposted in blue (8 kilometres) and yellow (11 kilometres), follow the same route as GR3 for a while.

The GR3 follows the Chemin des Buttes, tarmac at the beginning, which starts on the same side of the church. Further on, it becomes a road lined with new houses. The GR continues straight on and into the Chemin de Perrière opposite.

165

On the left is the starting point of a short-distance footpath, signposted in blue, which offers a very pleasant alternative to GR3 along the Cens; on the right is the start of a short-distance footpath signposted in yellow.

The GR3 continues straight on along the Chemin de Monteguerre, which begins as a tarmac road. Bear right at a fork. You will come to a road on the left.

8Km
2

The short-distance footpath, signposted in blue, starts on the left.

Pass through Montcellier.

The short-distance footpath, signposted in blue, links up on the left-hand side.

Take the first path on the right.

Detour
Continue along the road for 800 metres to the starting point of a short-distance footpath, currently being signposted in green.

The GR3 goes through La Magodière. The path bears left and leads to a junction; turn right, then take the first path on the left.

The short-distance footpath, signposted in yellow, which has followed the same route as GR3 from Orvault, carries straight on here.

When you come to the D26, turn left and then right on to a path; turn left at the fork. When you come to a road, turn right and follow it as far as a crossroads.

At this crossroads is the start and finish of a short-distance footpath (signposted in light blue); a section of which follows the same route as the yellow signposted walk from Orvault.

Turn left. A little way past La Guillaudière, when the road bears left, take a path on the right. This leads quickly downhill towards the Cens; cross the river by a footbridge and walk up the opposite side. Take a road on the right which becomes a dirt track. Walk along the edge of a tree nursery; at the end, turn sharp left and walk along the other edge.

Detour
Chapelle Notre-Dame-de-Bongarant
Elegant 15th century building, which still attracts many pilgrims each year.

Detour see left. Do not turn, but continue straight on; after 1 kilometre, you will come to the chapel of Notre-Dame-de-Bongarant (spelt Bon Garand on IGN map).

At La Tourie, you will come to a road; turn right on to it, then, at the next bend, turn on to the first path on the left. You will come to the N165;

ST-ÉTIENNE-DE-MONTLUC

Cordemais

les Moulins

la Peille

Merlet

le Goust

Marais de la Roche

les Rompuits

la Hurette

Moisonnais

la Haie Mériais

le Chaud

la Bessardais

Châtillon

Beauregard

la Basse Herlais

Bois de la Guignandière

le Douet Renard

St-Thomas

la Baie

le Champ Croulard

la Giquelais

la Bosse de la Giquelais

V. du Fresne

Kerrado

l'Oiselais

les Rouaudais

la Blardais

les Clunais

les Rouillonnais

Martinais

la Terrousais

l'Alma

la Milleterie

la Bretonnière

la Basse Bormaudérie

la Hô

Bel-Air

la Hériais

la Hardrais

le Guy Joli

Croulais

la Gentais

la Violais

la Coudre

la Colle

la Bahouinais

la Renaudais

la Gérardière

la Cr. Mortel

les Sables

les Prémions

la Masure

Bellevue

la H.

la Charpentrais

la Noë

Duret

St. P.

Pontreau

la Cr. Cottais

Forgerie

le Vivier

les Landes

la Haie des Bouillons

la Rivière

les Cernais

l'Angle

Chaussée

le Port

la Cavalnais

les Chevalerais

le Bas Vernet

la Rue

Simon

Venet

la Touche

l'Angle

le Couleyrou

les Mortiers

les Mortiers

la B.

les Giquelais

la Rue Blanche

Roche

Moricaud

le Bois

la Maillardière

la Noue de la Haie

Haut-Vent

la Lande Close

la Haie Mahéas Couv.

la Fenêtre

la Bérillais

le B. Pelletier

Audiais

la Folie

la Gaudinière

le Tertre

la Censive

la Nouë

la Poitie

le Chaud

la Vallais

la Gourche

la Colleterie

Chaugenet

Beauregard

Bellevue

l'Aubry

l'Aunay

la Gâtais

M. Neuf

le Barré

le Bois

la Chênaie

la Cloise Neuve

Chaussée

le Bois Alix

les Prioraïs

Cordemais

les Mariais

F.L.

IGN FRANCE 1723-1223

turn left and follow it for 20 metres as far as the crossroads.

NAUDIÈRES CROSSROADS

The GR3 crosses the Route Nationale and takes the path that leads diagonally off to the right. At the first crossroads, turn left. You will come to the expressway; cross over it on a road bridge a little further to the left. Immediately afterwards, take the road on the right and follow it for about 1 kilometre. When you come to the D81 turn left and then immediately right on to a dirt track. You will come to a road; turn left on to it and then immediately right on to another road; turn left again and then right into the hamlet of La Fontaine. At the junction, take the right-hand path. You will come to a road near La Petite Juliennais; turn left on to it, and then left again 300 metres further on at the crossroads; at the bottom of the hill, turn right on to the D17. Take the first path on the right leading up a small valley; as you come to a house, bear left on to a path, partly hidden from view, which leads across the small stream. Further on, continue along a good path which leads to the heights of the Sillon de Bretagne.

From here there is a view over the whole of the Loire estuary.

9Km
2:15

The Sillon de Bretagne is a long crystalline fold which, overlooking the lower Loire, stretches from Nantes to the Morbihan at La Roche-Bernard. It is, in fact, the most southerly of the main folds of the Massif Armoricain. It gives rise to a line of hills, many of them wooded, which the GR will follow for a long stretch before reaching La Brière.

Walk through La Roulerais and take the road on the left; you will soon come to a wayside shrine where you take the path on the right. Walk along the edge of a pond and head along the embankment towards the Château de la Juliennais; at the far end of the pond take the path on the left.

At this point, a short-distance footpath, signposted in blue and white, joins the GR from the right and follows the same route as far as

Cross a path and, near a wayside shrine, you will come into Saint-Etienne-de-Montluc via a recent housing development.

169

Saint-Etienne-de-Montluc.

SAINT-ETIENNE-DE-MONTLUC

Very ancient settlement, as demonstrated by a large menhir and many Celtic and Roman remains; the parish has existed since the Merovingian era. There was particular hostility here to the Revolution.

The footpath, signposted in blue and white, already mentioned above, continues straight on at this point. A walk of 5.5 kilometres, signposted in white and green, joins the GR along the same street and follows the same route as the GR for about the next 2 kilometres. These two short-distance footpaths can be used as alternatives to the GR.

**6.8Km
1:15**

On the right is the start of the short-distance footpath, signposted in white and green, mentioned above.

The GR3 does not go right into the centre of the town: shortly after you enter the town, turn right alongside a small manor house (Rue du Tertre-Blanc) towards La Gargouillère. Walk past Le Tertre-Blanc; at the top of the hill, turn left.

At the next junction take the road on the left which then bends to pass above the town before going down again. When you come to the Rue de Tivoli turn right into it. At the next crossroads, continue straight on along the Boulevard Alexandre-Goupil; at the next junction turn right towards the entrance to the cemetery and the sports hall; when the little road bears left towards the sports hall, take the footpath that starts opposite.

Caution: a little further on, after a junction where you continue straight on, turn right and virtually retrace your steps along a path which climbs slowly and then heads off again in a generally westerly direction. At the top of the hill you will come to a road.

Turn left on to this road, and, when it bears left, turn right along a small path through the trees. Carry straight on over meadows and woods for about 1.3 kilometres, then turn right on to a path leading to the top of the ridge and a minor road near La Primaudière farm leading in the direction of Les Hunaudais; beyond the farm, the road becomes a path lined with hedges that you follow along the top of the ridge for 1.5 kilometres until you reach the hamlet of La Colle (in the distance, you will see the coal-fired thermal power station of Cordemais). Go down the road on the left, and, after the bend, turn right on to another minor road, which soon turns left. At this point turn off it on to the path that continues following the hillside of the Sillon de Bretagne. Soon you will come to a road; take the path starting virtually opposite. You will cross another road and then come to the junction with the D49.

Junction of GR3 with the D49
Detour
LA CROIX MORZEL

Detour see left. Turn left on to the D49; after 600 metres you will come to the D17 and 150 metres further along the D49 to the Cordemais SNCF station.

The GR crosses the D49 and then three more roads: each time continue straight on, the fourth time along a path that is tarmac to begin with (passage J. de Montauban) and leads through the hamlet of Le Goust. When you reach a Y-shaped junction, take the right-hand fork that will take you back to the top of the ridge from which you have gradually been moving away. Turn left when you come to a wood; the path continues to climb, then levels out and finally joins a broad path at a bend; turn left on to this path. Leave it when it bears left and continue on the other side of a fence along a path on the edge of the woods. This joins a road at a bend; turn left on to the road. At the top of the hill, turn left on to a path and, immediately afterwards, take the left-hand fork. At a Y-shaped junction, 800 metres further on, take the right-hand fork.

8.5Km
2:15

At a road junction, take the road that continues straight on towards La Touche and becomes a path on leaving the village; take the path on the left after the last house. A little further on, at a fork near a large modern house, take the right-hand fork. Further on, at the junction of three paths on the edge of a wood, take the one on the far right. You will come to a road junction; take the road on the far left leading to L'Orme. Past the hamlet it becomes a wide tarmac path leading to La Coudre. At the cluster of houses on the edge La Coudre, turn left. The path goes downhill, skirts a pond and ends up at the D17. Turn right and follow it for 500 metres along its former route that is no longer used by vehicles. You will now be close to a crossroads.

CROSSROADS
L'ANGELLERAIS

Before the crossroads the GR3 turns right on to a path that goes up towards L'Angelleraye (spelling on the road sign: the bus stop and

IGN map both have 'L'Angellerais'); at the entrance to the village, carry straight on along a path (north), ignoring the chain that is sometimes found across the start of the path.

When you reach the top of the hill, turn left on to the road that passes close to a restored mill. At the crossroads carry straight on along a path heading towards Le Vivier. After you have left the hamlet, and, where the path bends to the left to go down towards the D17, take another path on the right that goes downhill much more slowly. When you reach the D17, turn right on to its old route, then take the first path on the right; this will take you back to the top of the ridge. You will come to a road: turn left on to it, then, almost immediately, turn off it on to a path; when this joins another path, turn right and pick up the same road at La Gouairie. Turn left, then left again at the next crossroads and then right along the first street, which becomes a path; carry straight on to the lake of La Vallée Mabile.

5.5Km
1:30

LAC DE LA VALLÉE MABILE

⌂ Å Y

1.8Km
0:30

The GR turns off the path leading to the car park and camp site on to a small tree-lined path leading to the edge of the lake; follow it as far as the dam. From here, steps lead down to the bottom of the valley; walk along it to the D17, where you turn right and walk to Savenay.

SAVENAY

⌂ ✗ Y ⚏ ⇢ ⇥

Dolmen Roman road from Nantes to La Roche-Bernard passed through town. Many Frankish and Breton coins from Merovingian period have been found here. Remained a monarchist stronghold during the Revolution. Scene of many disturbances until the end of 1793, when on 24 December, the last major battle of the Wars of the Vendée was fought there.

At the first fork, on the edge of Savenay, the GR bears slightly to the right (signposted 'Le Lac'). If you bear left instead, you will come to the SNCF station (1.1 kilometres).

The Rue de l'Hôpital leads to the Place de la Balance. Carry on along the Rue Madame-Jan virtually opposite. At the end of this street bear left (Rue de l'Eglise), then right (Rue de Saint-Nazaire) which leads to the coach station. The GR then takes a road slightly to the right (Rue du Maréchal-Juin). Walk under the express-way, across the D17 and continue along a path offset slightly to the left. Turn left before the first building in Le Matz. A little further on you will come to the edge of Le Haut Matz. Turn right, then immediately left on to a path leading up a small valley to the hamlet of La

15.7Km
4

Vallée Mismi. As you leave the hamlet, cross the D93 and then take the first path on the right (hidden by a house). Further on, it bends to the left and joins a road; turn left and walk along the railway line for 500 metres. Cross the railway line and, immediately afterwards, at the fork, take the left-hand road towards La Berthelais. Once you have passed Le Berthelais, carry on and then, just before the expressway, turn right. At a crossroads, 1.3 kilometres further on, take the wide path on the right. When it ends, turn left (chemin des Roussinettes). You will come to a road; turn right, then left as you approach the railway line. Beyond Le Bas-Vérac, the road becomes a path along the railway line; cross over at the level crossing and turn left on to a road. A little further on, turn right on to the path leading into the wood (Bois du Rocher).

On your way through this wood, you will cross an ancient Gallic road near an IGN altitude indicator.

On leaving the wood, turn left and then left again at a crossroads; turn right at the first road, which becomes a path. This ends at a road, where you turn left. Turn right before the railway line, then left on to the first path that crosses it and heads towards a mill. At the end of the path, take the fork to the right before the hamlet, turn right at the fork and left where the paths cross. Take the road to the left. When you come to the D204, cross over and turn on to a path at right angles to the road. When you come to a road, turn right. At the second crossroads you will be at La Norielle.

La Norielle

Alternative route On the left is the start of the Bois-Joubert alternative route (see page 179).

The GR3 goes through La Savinais and then comes to Treffier; coming out of the hamlet, turn left on to a path which, a little further on, crosses a road to reach La Morandais.

4.6Km
1:05

In the hamlet, turn right on a road, then take the first path to the left, which, a little further on, leads along a stretch of marshland where herons can often be seen.

Cross the N773 and carry on along the path opposite; a little further on, turn left on to a path (barely visible under a hedge). Walk along further stretches of marshland to a wide

path; turn left and cross the Canal de la Chaussée. Just a little further on you will come to La Brière.

La Brière
Detour *15 mins*
BESNÉ
🍷 ⛴ 🚂 ═══
Turn right on to D204; 300 metres further on you will come to the centre of Besné.

4.6Km
1:10

Turn left on to the D204, cross the railway line and the Brivet. When the road bears left, turn off it to the right. This road turns left, right and left again. At the second right-hand bend, take the path on the left, which soon bears right. When you come to a road, turn right towards La Lande. Shortly after the entrance to the village, turn left on to another road; at the T-junction, take the road on the left; at the Y-junction, take the road on the right. At the next road junction, bear left. You will come to a larger road; at the next junction, turn left. You are now at Le Rocher.

Le Rocher
Detour *55 mins*
PONTCHÂTEAU
🏨 🍴 🍷 ⛴ 🚂 ═══
If you turn right instead and walk for 3.5 kilometres, you will come to Pontchâteau.

3.5Km
0:55

The GR continues along the road to Cuhin and turns left on to a minor road which soon turns right. At Callac you will come to the D16; turn left on to it, then turn right towards Le Buisson Rond; 500 metres further on, at the fork, take the left-hand road. After a short while, at a pond, take the minor road on the right which leads past a group of houses and then becomes a path. At the spot where a path turns off to the right, continue straight on (no signposting). At this point, you are entering the Brière National Park; the GR3 does not leave the park until it ends, just before reaching Guérande. Further on, turn sharp left. You will come to Les Métairies.

Les Métairies
Detour *10 mins*
CHÂTEAU DU DEFFAY
⛺ 🍴
Turn right and, 500 metres further on, across D33.

0.5Km
0:05

Carry straight on along the minor road you have joined; when it ends, turn left on to another road; a little further on turn right on to a path. At this junction, the GR is joined by the alternative route.

Junction

Opposite is the junction with a short-distance footpath, signposted in green and white, which will follow the same route as GR3 as far as Le Haut-Bergon.

Alternative route from Bois-Joubert (see pages 179–183).

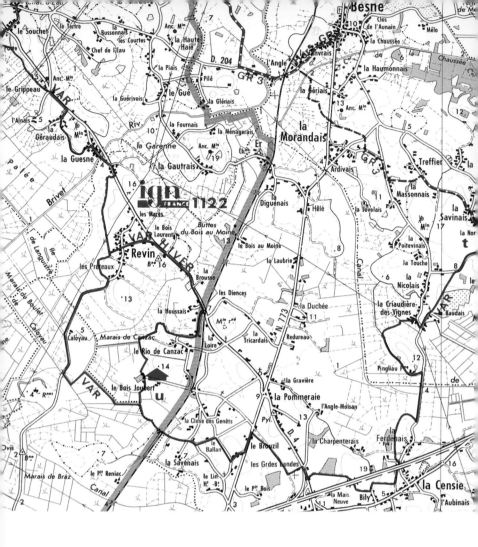

The fauna of Brière

The marshes of Bois-Joubert and Caloyau often provide the silent, attentive walker with opportunities to observe a large number of birds and mammals. In addition to the 39 species of nesting birds, some of which can be seen frequently (herons, buzzards, ducks), there are many migratory birds (snipe, curlews, tits). Nineteen species of mammals inhabit the area around the GR. Coypu (often to be seen swimming) dig burrows in which unwary hikers can fall and twist their ankles, while musk rats block paths with their lairs.

The Bois-Joubert Alternative Route

From La Norielle to Les Métairies – 24 kilometres. La Brière is not easily accessible: marshes and canals act as barriers to walkers. Nevertheless, the imminent opening of a Nature Centre on the Bois-Joubert estate, part of which will provide overnight accommodation for hikers, has encouraged attempts to find routes linking up with the GR3 so that walkers can benefit from the resources offered by the new centre. Regular flooding in winter, caused by changes in ground water levels, means that, in places, only tarred roads are passable, and it was hardly feasible to create a GR that could be used only for a few weeks each year.

Thus the proposed itinerary is an harmonious compromise. Depending on the season, those in charge of the Bois-Joubert estate will suggest unsignposted alternative routes.

La Brière changes with the seasons; in midwinter, the marshes become huge lakes, which are strewn at the beginning of spring with a mass of raised islands – a paradise for bird lovers. We highly recommend walking several times along this route, in different seasons. Each season offers its own charms and new opportunities for exploration.

Eventually, this alternative route may well become part of a new GR, currently on the drawing board, that will take hikers on a tour of the Guérlande peninsula.

The first part of the alternative route, east of Bois-Joubert, leads along the edge of Pingliau marshes and those of Bois-Joubert and is passable in all seasons. A rather lengthy stretch of tarmac road between the two marshes, made necessary by the proximity of the Nantes-Saint-Nazaire expressway, is offset to a large extent by the splendour of the preceding and following sections.

The second part, to the west and north of Bois-Joubert, begins by crossing a stretch of marshland, an unforgettable experience for those of us who have done it. For those who are quiet and patient, there are frequent opportunities to see birds and small mammals. Despite a considerable amount of improvement work (footbridges), with which local people and walkers from Paris have assisted, this section is passable for only about six months every year, but a diversion (not signposted for the time being) is shown on the map. After that, good paths linking plots of agricultural land and affording clear views over the marshes are passable all year round.

Short-distance footpaths starting from the gîte will be suggested. In summer, when the marshes are accessible, you are strongly recommended to devote a day to them, since they will give you a greater insight into the marshlands than that afforded by the GR. Since the itineraries are dependent on water levels, all relevant information will be provided at the gîte. The IGN 1/50,000 map of the 'Parc de Brière' is highly recommended.

 La Norielle

Turn off the GR3 to the right, along the road which bears right, then left and right again. At this last bend, leave the road and follow a path that continues straight on. You will come to a road, where you turn right; at the end of this road, turn right and turn left at the next junction. Walk through La Criaudière des Vignes; the road continues along a path leading round a farm, La gagnerie de Pingliau. A 'gagnerie' is that part of an island or

peninsula in the marshes given over to crop cultivation.

After Pingliau farm you will come to a road where you turn right to cross the marsh. Once across the marsh, turn right on to a wide path that very soon bears right. As you approach the expressway, turn left on to a road, then right and walk under the bridge.

4 Km
1:05

La Sencie

(Censie on the IGN map)
On the expressway, 'La Sencie' stop for TTO bus services, nos 50 and 53 from Nantes to Piriac or Le Croisic via Saint-Nazaire and La Baule; only those services that do not make the detour via Donges; in the opposite direction, the bus stop is on the other carriageway of the expressway, 300 metres further on.

5Km
1:15

Immediately after the bridge, bear right, and, at the next junction, turn right and once again walk under the expressway, then turn left. You will come to the D4. On the left, at the crossroads, the 'Six Croix' stop for TTO bus services, same numbers as at La Sencie, but this time only those services that do make the detour via Donges.

Turn right on to the D4, then turn left on to the first road; turn right, then left towards Le Brouzil and then, before the first houses, turn right on to a path (small stone wayside shrine at the junction). When you come to a road, turn left. At a fork, take the road on the right, then on the bend turn left on to a tarmac path, which crosses the railway line further on. Turn right along the railway line, then left on to the first path which, later on, bends and skirts the marshes. At the end of the path, continue straight on, keeping a small canal on the right of you. Under some trees you will pick up a path. It bends to the right along a fence, then left alongside a stretch of water and leads to the estate of Bois-Joubert.

DOMAINE DE BOIS-JOUBERT

There are no shops within a reasonable distance.
A network of short-distance footpaths is being laid out, together with a circuit for

Caution. For a little more than a kilometre, the alternative route beyond the estate of Bois-Joubert is passable for only about six months of the year. In winter, use the detour (not currently signposted) marked on the map.

On leaving the estate of Bois-Joubert, retrace your steps by turning right towards the

181

bird-watchers.
If arrangements are made in advance, an official of the Society for the Study and Protection of Nature in Brittany, which owns the premises, will be able to help you observe the wild animals and birds in the area.
A nature centre is being set up.

On the right is the starting point of the second part of the alternative route.

marshes over which you arrived. Walk along a small canal for 100 metres. Near an old lock, you will come to another small canal at right angles.

Walk along the dyke between two small canals. One of them leads off to the left. Keep the other one on your right-hand side all the time. When another canal blocks your way, turn left and walk along it. Just before the Canal de Caloyau, a footbridge, built for the GR, leads over it; on the other side of the bridge, continue straight on along the Canal de Caloyau towards the minor road which you will reach after crossing a small ditch, again over a footbridge built for the GR. Turn right on to this road and continue between two tamarisk hedges past Caloyau farm.

14.5Km
3:40

When the road begins to turn away from the marsh, turn left at the corner of a house on to a path linking various plots of land. The path skirts the marsh and leads to a minor road; turn left; 20 metres further on it bears right, but you turn off it and continue straight on along another path. You will come to the D4 at La Guesné: turn left and follow it for 100 metres, then turn left on to the old road. At the village cross turn left (note the cottages). The path leads to another path where you turn right along the edge of the marshes. You will come to La Géraudais: turn right and rejoin the D4, where you turn left and follow the road for 300 metres. At a crossroads, turn left, then immediately right on to the path leading behind the farm. At some houses, a kilometre further on, turn right.

Detour *40 mins*
Le Pont Brûlé

Detour see left. If you turn left instead of right, a good path, passable in all seasons, will lead through the heart of the marsh, to the Pont Brûlé. From here you have excellent views over the marshes and islands and also over a long stretch of the Canal de Coulaie. You may see cattle being transported on punts.

You will come to the D4 100 metres further on. Turn right on to it, and then immediately left to walk through Le Souchet and La Maison (fine cottages). Opposite the water tower, turn left, then, on a bend, bear right on to a path that is tarmac to begin with. You will cross one of the highest points in the region (altitude: 20 metres). At the end of the path, turn left.

Caution. In this section, from La Maison Neuve to the GR3, the network of paths was completely changed in 1981; as a result, the maps are totally inaccurate.

One kilometre further on, at the end of the path, turn left on to the road and then, 100 metres further on, turn on to a path which leads after a kilometre to the D16. Turn right and follow this road for 200 metres, then turn left. Pass through Bout de Ville and Coëmeux (spelled Coimeux on the IGN map), take the first path on the right and then the first on the left; at the end of this path the Bois-Joubert alternative route rejoins the GR3.

Turn right for Savenay, left for La Gravelais to continue to Guérande.

Junction GR3

183

Junction

2.5Km
0:40

At the end of the path turn left on to a road. Further on, 100 metres, turn right, and then right again on to a path.

Walk past two mills; the path becomes a minor road and comes to the D33.

D33
Detour *10 mins*
SAINTE-REINE-DE-BRETAGNE
✕ ☉ ⌨
Turn right on to the D33 and follow it for 800 metres.

4.7Km
1:10

The GR3 crosses the D33 and, 800 metres further on, turns left on to a path. When it comes to an end, take the road on the right and then the first on the left. At a group of houses, bear right along the Rue des Cormiers. When you reach L'Organais, turn left and immediately right into the Rue des Cerisiers. The road is tarmac as far as Crévy farm, where it becomes a path. Turn left at the first path and continue to le Haut-Bergon.

The short-distance footpath mentioned above turns left on to the D4.

Cross the D4 and continue straight on along the Rue des Raquettes which, once past the houses, becomes a wide path. After a small poplar wood, turn right on to a path. It will take you to La Gravelais.

LA GRAVELAIS
☉

Turn right in to the main street, then turn left towards the dolmen.

Detour *45 mins*
LA CROIX DE COËTQUEN
✕ ☉
▬▬

3Km
0:45

Detour see left. Continue straight on along the main road of La Gravelais; cross D4 and continue down the road opposite, the Rue de Bercéhan. Further on, at the corner of a pond, take the Rue des Joncs; carry straight on along the path, cross the D2 and continue straight on along the minor road which passes Coëtquen. You will come to the N165, the Nantes-Vannes expressway at La Croix de Coëtquen. To cross the expressway, turn right 150 metres before La Croix de Coëtquen and go through the underpass.

The GR3 takes you past the beautiful dolmen of La Roche-aux-Loups, turns right and a little further on, crosses over a canal. It takes the first path on the right, then the next on the left.

A short-distance footpath (7.5 kilometres), signposted in blue, joins the GR here and follows the same route for 1.5 kilometres.

When you come to a minor road, take the path that leads diagonally off to the left and, at the end of it, continue along the Rue du Trélan. Turn right opposite a pond. You are now at Trélan.

185

Trélan
Detour *10 mins*
LA CHAPELLE-DES-MARAIS
🍴 🍷 🏛 🚃

The short-distance footpath continues straight on; follow it for 500 metres.

At this point you will join the short-distance footpath again as it joins the GR on the left from the centre of la Chapelle-des-Marais.

Cross the D50 (Rue de la Saulzaie) and continue straight on. Turn right at the end of the path.

Take the second road on the left (Rue de la Surbinais).

The short-distance footpath continues straight on. The Rue de la Surbinais ends at the Rue du Gué; turn right and at the end of the road

There are many megaliths in this area and they are the origin of many legends. The remains of jewellery and tools that have been found are evidence of a major prehistoric settlement in the

you will join the D2, which crosses a small canal; turn immediately left Further on, turn left to continue along the edge of Gué marsh. The path bears right and, 600 metres further on, comes to an area of dense gorse thickets on the right; here, a path on the right leads to the D2, where you turn left. Cross another canal.

At the fork at Sapin Vert, the GR bears left.

10.8Km
2:35

region, which, at that time, was not marshland but densely-wooded hills and valleys.

The footpath, signposted in white, that joins the GR along the right-hand fork is a short-distance footpath of 20 kilometres (may be shortened to 16 or 13 kilometres) which will follow the same route as the GR for almost 4 kilometres.

When you reach La Ville Rio, turn left. At Le Haut-Langâtre, the road turns left; continue straight on along the tarmac path. At the next junction, turn right to walk round Thora marshes.

These marshes, like others on the route taken by the GR, vary greatly according to the season: in winter, when the ground water rises, they are lakes; in summer, they can take on

The flat-bottomed punts of the Brière, with their tapering ends, are known as 'chalands'. They are built in various sizes, for the transport of people or cattle or for hunting. For a long time, these vessels were the main method of transport in the region, particularly before the recent construction of roads. The vessels are still very much in use and are carefully maintained; they are propelled and steered by means of a pole, which is not as simple as it looks . . . A journey by punt, whatever the season, is never monotonous for those who use their eyes and ears.

Punts in the Brière region

The short-distance footpath, signposted in white, turns off to the right here.

Detour 15 mins
Château de Ranrouët
12th and 17th century. All that remains of this ancient fortress are the moat, entrance gate flanked by two

the appearance of ordinary pasture land, strewn with numerous clumps of reeds. When you come to a small road, turn left on to it. At Sapilon, turn left on to a good tarmac path.

The GR crosses the D33 and carries straight on, then takes the second path on the right which leads up the slope of the butte de Guélan.

189

towers and outer walls reinforced by four circular towers. Some restoration work is in progress. Continue straight on for 1 kilometre.

The first wide tarmac path forms part of the route of a short-distance footpath, signposted in dark green, which follows the same itinerary as the GR3 for 4 kilometres; it is part of a 9 kilometres walk.

When the path comes to an end, take the road opposite. Follow the D51 through Hoscas.

AU BIGNON D'HOSCAS

⌂

Junction with GR39 coming from la Roche-Bernard to the north.

You will see some fine cottages in the typical style of the Brière region; at the corner of one of them, turn left on to a tarmac path. When the path bears left, take the right-hand path. Turn left, then right and jump over a small ditch; you are now at the port of Hoscas, which is typical of the ports in the area, and you will have a splendid view over the marshes of Grande Brière. Continue along the edge of the marshes until you come to a good path which you should follow. At the next fork, continue straight on and join a minor road.

Detour

100 metres to the left there is a fine view from the wooded path over La Curée; the view stretches over the entire marsh of Grande Brière, as far as the belfry of Saint-Joachim.

The GR3 follows the road round to the left. A little further on you will cross under the D47. When you come to Marlais, turn left on to the D51.

6Km
1:30

The short-distance footpath, signposted in dark green, turns right.

Walk through La Chapelle and, on leaving the hamlet, turn right onto the minor road leading to Les Fraîches, which soon becomes a good path; continue along it for 1 kilometre. You will come to another good path; turn left and follow it for 1.5 kilometres. This Chemin Pavé, or Chemin des Saulniers, is an ancient Roman road.

If you turn right instead, you will find yourself on a link route (1.2 kilometres) leading to a 7 kilometres walk signposted in bright green.

Cross the D83 at Le Pigeon Blanc.

Le Pigeon Blanc
Detour *15 mins*
SAINT-LYPHARD
⛺ 🍷 ♨

The places known as 'Pigeon' are often close to ancient settlements. It is thought they are the result of a linguistic confusion between 'columba' (dove) and 'colubra' (snake); these place names may well be associated with the local legends, derived from the myth of Melusina, in which snakes play an important role.

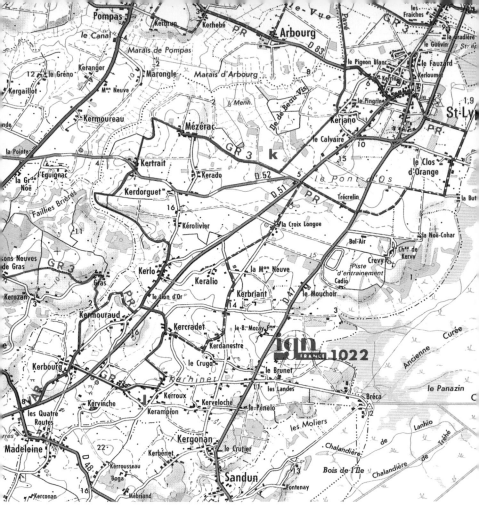

The rights of the people of La Brière

These customary rights date back at least to the time of the Merovingians; they were confirmed by a decree issued by François II on 8 August 1461 and in a charter granted by Louis XVI on 12 November 1784; they were also recognized by the Revolutionary government (decrees of 1791 and 1792). They are unique in France. La Grande Brière is the joint property of the 17 parishes (nowadays 21 communes) that surround it and is managed by a syndic established by Louis-Philippe. In consequence, it is not a part of any local authority district, nor has it ever belonged to any lord of the manor; rather, it belongs to every inhabitant of the district, all of whom are entitled to cut peat from it. The people of the region are their own masters, and are deeply rooted in their native district; since time immemorial, these rights have been vigorously defended, by armed insurrection if necessary, as was the case between 1820 and 1833. The marshlands of Donges and Le Haut-Brivet have slightly different statutes, and two different governing bodies.

From the church belfry there is a magnificent view over la Grande Brière. Turn left on to the D83 and follow it for 1 kilometre to the centre of Saint-Lyphard.

A 12 kilometres short-distance footpath, signposted in white joins the GR here; like the GR, it leads from Saint-Lyphard to Kerhinet and for 9 kilometres follows the same route.

Detour
Le Pont d'Os
A local tradition links this curious name with a battle against an enemy, possibly the Romans. The story goes that there were so many dead that a bridge was built from their bones (over the stream, according to one version, and across the marshes according to another).
A short distance to the left is the pont d'Os (Bone Bridge).

9.7Km
2:10

The short-distance footpath, signposted in white, continues straight on.

The GR is joined by a short-distance footpath of 9 kilometres, signposted in green, coming from Saint-Lyphard. It may be used as a shorter alternative to GR3; it passes through the Clos d'Orange, from where there is a view over the marshes of La Grande Brière and where barge trips may be possible. It follows the same route as the GR as far as Kerhinet.

The GR3 continues along the minor road opposite. At the hamlet of Kerjano, bear right; at the end of the road, turn right.

The GR3 goes through the hamlet of Mézérac, where there are fine examples of the local houses. The road turns right and after the bend, before the last house the GR takes the left-hand path which leads down to Mézérac marshes. Turn left and walk along the edge of the marsh. Take the first path on the left towards Kertrait. Cross the D52 and, immediately after the pond, take the path on the right and turn right at the end; the path bears left when it returns to the marsh. You will come to a road: turn right and walk into Kerlo, a village with some fine cottages. Turn left 500 metres further on.

Cross the D51; you will come to Kercradet, another village with cottages.

Turn right and then, 300 metres further on, left. You will come to the village of Kerhinet.

193

KERHINET

⌂ ⌂ ✕ 𝖸

Local museum (highly
recommended) and
exhibitions. Village of typical
cottages restored by the
Regional Park authorities.

The GR is joined again by
the short-distance footpath,
signposted in white,
mentioned above.

Detour
Megalithic burial

The GR3 follows the main street through the
village (closed to motor vehicles), then turns
right on to the road. Walk through Kerverné.

Detour see left. Before reaching D51, turn left
on to a path running alongside La Motte mill;

chambers

Local tradition has it that the imprint of a body is visible on the tombstone in the first chamber.

150 metres away on the right is a fine megalithic burial chamber: 50 metres further on, on the left, there is another, less well-preserved tomb. The two tombs are said to be connected by a tunnel filled with gold; however, this disappears as soon as digging starts! Further on, 500 metres west, is 'Gargantua's pebble', a menhir of white quartz almost two metres high.

The GR3 crosses the D51 and enters Kerbourg, another village typical of the region.

Kerbourg

Exactly half-way between the megalithic complexes of Arbourg and Guérande; this fact is sometimes used to support a theory that the megaliths served as landmarks along long-distance paths.

The following section of the GR3, fording the marshes, is one of the most beautiful and wildest sections of the GR3 in Loire-Atlantique. It is impassable in winter and an alternative route is given.

Alternative route to Bouzaire In case of floods, do not turn right in Kerbourg on to the road, but turn left and continue to the D51. Then turn right on to the D48. You rejoin the GR3 at Bouzaire, where you turn left on to it.

12.2Km
3:05

At Kerbourg the GR3 turns right on to the road and then, shortly afterwards, left on to a path, which bears right. Be careful, because a little further on the GR suddenly turns off this path on to a less obvious path leading to the Pont des Romains or Pont de Gras; this bridge will take you over a marsh.

Opposite is the starting point for the short-distance

Continue opposite into Gras. Take the road to the right, then immediately an agricultural farm

---

The traditional houses of the Brière

The front of each unit has a door, a dormer window providing access to the attic and (if the house is under 200 years old) a window. The room occupies an area of about 50 metres square, is barely 2 metres high and the walls may be 80 cm thick. Each house may be made up of one or several units forming a small terrace; there may also be extensions, possibly at an angle to the main building, lower, windowless buildings used as sheds. The wooden frame of the roof is covered with reeds, which may be up to one metre thick. The walls are made of stone, bonded with a mixture of clay and reeds; in certain areas they are whitewashed. A little late in the day, building regulations have been laid down to ensure that new buildings blend in with the older dwellings: thatched roofs have become obligatory in certain locations.

Guérande

Visit the ramparts, the Porte Saint-Michel, which now houses the museum of old Guérande, the church of Saint-Aubin (12th and 16th centuries), the 17th and 18th century houses and the neighbouring salt marshes. Guérande was already in existence during the Gallo-Roman period, when it was the meeting place for three roads. From the 12th to the 14th centuries, the history of Guérande was fairly eventful: it belonged alternately to the Bretons, the English and the French. In 1386 it finally became part of the Duchy of Brittany, which, in turn, became a French province in 1532. The period of the Revolution was relatively calm, since the town, unlike neighbouring towns in the region, tended to support the Republican cause, but it was occupied by Royalists for two weeks in 1793. Balzac's novel *Beatrix* contributed a great deal to the fame of the town.

footpath, signposted in white, that has already been mentioned.

track on the left. Continue straight ahead until you reach a marshy area and bear left along the side of it. Further on, the path leaves the marshy area. At the end of the track, turn right. At the next junction, turn left on to another track. Cross a road near Maisons Neuves de Gras. Carry straight on. Take the D48 to the right; further on turn off it on to a broad track to the left. The GR goes up on to a bank round the Kercabus lake. You will come to Bouzeray; turn right, and, 200 metres further on, turn left and then left again. You will come to a road, which you follow. This soon joins another road; cross it and continue along a path. Bear left, then right and at the entrance to the Bréhadour Municipal camp site, take a road to the right. Cross the Guérande bypass and enter the town along the Rue du Parc Savary. Continue along the Rue du Sénéchal; at the end of the road, turn left, then right into the Avenue Anne-de-Bretagne.

GUÉRANDE

Salt marshes near Guérande

ACCOMMODATION GUIDE

The many different kinds of accommodation in France are explained in the introduction. Here we include a selection of hotels and other addresses, which is by no means exhaustive—the hotels listed are usually in the one-star or two-star categories. We have given full postal addresses where available so bookings can be made.

There has been an explosive growth in bed and breakfast facilities (chambres d'hôte) in the past few years, and staying in these private homes can be especially interesting and rewarding. Local shops and the town hall (mairie) can usually direct you to one.

Abbaye de Saint Maur
⌂
☎ 41.80.50.96

Amboise
37400 Amboise
(H) Choiseul
36 Quai Charles Guinot
☎ 47.30.45.45
(H) Bellevue
12 Quai Charles Guinot
☎ 47.57.02.26

Ancenis
44150 Ancenis
(H) Les Voyageurs
98 rue Georges Clemenceau
☎ 40.83.10.06

Angers
49000 Angers
⌂ du Lac de Maine
☎ 41.48.57.01
⌂
rue Darwin
☎ 41.48.14.55 .

Beaulieu sur Layon
⌂
Rue du Dolmen
☎ 41.78.40.56
⌂ communal
Mme Beduneau
☎ 41.78.31.77
Mr Clément
☎ 41.78.38.74
or 41.78.34.02
(H)
Mr Coiffard

35 rue Saint Vincent
☎ 41.78.64.44

Beaumont en Véron
⌂ Les Coudreaux
☎ 47.27.56.10

Beuil en Touraine
⌂ La Solivière
☎ 47 27.56.10

Bignon d'Hoscas
⌂ Maison de la nature
et de la randonnée de Brière
⌂ 40.91.33.91

Blaison
⌂ Cheman
Mme Antoine
☎ 41.57.17.60

Blaison Gohier
49320 Brissac Quince
⌂ Lo Bois Brincon
Mr Cailleau
☎ 41.57.17.88

Blois
⌂ CRJS
Chemin Saint Georges
☎ 54.43.99.73

Boulancourt
77632 Larchant
⌂
☎ 64.37.47.15
⌂
Mr Creuzet
☎ 64.24.10.43

Bouzille
49530 Lire
⌂ La Guichetiere
Mr Thiau
☎ 40.98.11.79
⌂
Mme Francoise Gaudin
14 rue des aires
☎ 40.98.13.08

Briarres sur Essonne
45390 Puiseaux
⌂
☎ 38.39.13.59

Buthiers
77760 La Chapelle la Reine
⌂ de Buthiers
☎ 64.24.12.87

Le Cellier
(H) des voyageurs
☎ 40.25.40.03
(H) de la terrasse
☎ 40.25.31.00

Chalonnes sur Loire
(H) Hotel de France
5 rue Nationale
☎ 41.78.00.12

Champtoceaux
⌂
Mme Lhoste
15 rue Jean V
☎ 40.83.55.60
(H) de la Cote
2 rue du Docteur giffard
☎ 40.83.50.39

ACCOMMODATION GUIDE

⌂ chez Claudie
Le Club du Moulin
☎ 40.83.50.43
⌂ des voyageurs
Place de l'église
☎ 40.83.50.09

Chancay
⌂ Vallée de Vaux
☎ 47.27.56.10

La Chapelle sur Erdre
⌂ de Nantes
2 place de la Manu
☎ 40.20.57.25

Charnizay
⌂ La Tauchonnerie
☎ 47.27.56.10

Chécy
45430 Chécy
⌂ de la Diligence
☎ 38.86.95.09

Cheille
⌂ Les Maisons Rouges
☎ 47.27.56.10

Chemille sur Indrois
⌂ Le Bourg
☎ 47.27.56.10

Chénehuttes Trèves Cunault
⌂ Beauregard
Mr F.Tonnelier
☎ 41.67.92.93

Cheverny
41700 Contres
⌂
Mr Bernard Gerard
☎ 54.79.62.41

Chilleurs aux Bois
⌂ de Chamerolles
☎ 38.39.80.99
or 16.42 60.68.02

Combleux
45530 Vitry aux loges
⌂ de la Marine
☎ 38.84.12.69
or 38.83.16.03

Denée
⌂ La Boule d'or
☎ 41.78.72.46

Donges
44480 Donges
⌂ Le Bois Joubert

Mr Gourrand Yann
☎ 40.91.01.10

Donnery
45450 Fay aux Loges
⌂ donnery
☎ 38.59.20.10
or 38.59.27.48
⌂
2 rue de la Bretonnerie
☎ 38.62.04.88

Epigne les Bois
⌂ La Cage
☎ 47.27.56.10

Estouy
45300 Pithiviers
⌂ de la Vallée
6 rue du Vau
☎ 38.34.20.83
⌂
Mlle Roy
☎ 38.34.20.44
or 38.34.20.61
⌂
Mr Clouzeau
☎ 38.34.20.13
or 38.83.96.36

Fay aux loges
⌂ Le poisson d'argent
☎ 38.59.56.28

Fleury les Aubrais
⌂ de la Brossette
☎ 38.75.00.36

Fontevrault l'Abbaye
⌂ Abbaye Royale
Mme Foucault
☎ 41.51.73.52
⌂ La Croix Blanche
☎ 41.51.71.11

Gennes
⌂ Hostellerie de la Loire
9 rue des Cadets de Saumur
☎ 41.51.81.03
⌂ Aux naulets d'Anjou
18 rue Croix de Mission
☎ 41.51.81.88

La Guichetière
⌂
Chez Mr Thiau
☎ 40.98.11.79

Haut des Bruyères
45450 Fay aux Loges
⌂ Maison Forestiere
☎ 38.57.13.02

Herbignac
44410 Herbignac
⌂ Le Bignon d'Hoscas
☎ 40.91.33.91

Lac de la Vallée Mobile
⌂ Le relais du Lac
☎ 40.58.32.78

Langeais
⌂
☎ 47.96.74.76

Launay
⌂ Chateau de Lanay
☎ 41.59.13.03

Malesherbes
⌂
Lieu dit le Couvent
Route de Pinson
☎ 38.34.84.18

Mareau au Bois
45300 Pithiviers
⌂ de la Motte
☎ 38.34.11.74 ·
⌂ du Domaine Résidentiel
de Chamerolles
☎ 38.35.80.99
or 16.1.42.60.68.02

Martigne Briand
⌂
Mr Rochais
Place du 11 Novembre
☎ 41.59.43.72
⌂
Mr Jean Matignon
rue du 8 Mai
☎ 41.59.44.71

Meung sur Loire
⌂
☎ 38.44.75.85
⌂ Pierre Gailly
rue de Chateaudun
☎ 38.44.36.39

Montjeau sur loire
⌂ de la Loire
2 quai des mariniers
☎ 41.39.80.20

Montlouis sur Loire
⌂ Husseau
☎ 47.27.56.10
⌂ La Ville
Place de la Mairie
☎ 47.50.84.84

Montsoreau

Ⓗ Le Bussy
☎ 41.51.70.18
◠ Atelier Mirador
Mr priou
Qaui A. Dumas
☎ 41.51.75.33

Moulin de Franconville
45390 Puiseaux
◠
Mr Coulon
☎ 38.39.13.59

Nantes
44000 Nantes
◠ Beaulieu
9 Boulevard Vincent Gache
☎ 40.47.91.64
◠ Porte Neuve
1 rue Porte Neuve
☎ 40.20.00.80
◠ de l'Edit de Nantes
1 rue de Gigant
☎ 40.73.41.46

Neuille
49680 Vivy
◠ La Poitivinière
Mr Louveau
☎ 41.52.55.08

Orléans
45000 Orléans
◠ de la Motte Sanguin
☎ 38.87.60.06
◠ d'Orléans
14 faubourg de la madeleine
☎ 38.62.45.75
Ⓗ Les 4 saisons
351 rue de la reine blanche
☎ 38.66.14.30
Ⓗ d'arc
37 rue de la République
☎ 38.53.10.94
Ⓗ Les Cèdres
17 rue Marechal Foch
☎ 38.62.22.92
Ⓗ Novotel
12 rue Honoré de Balzac
☎ 38.63.04.28
Ⓗ d'Orléans
6 rue Adolphe Crespin
☎ 38.53.35.34
Ⓗ Saint Aignon
3 place Gambetta
☎ 38.53.15.35
Ⓗ Sofitel
☎ 38. 62.17.39
Ⓗ Terminus
40 rue de la République
☎ 38.53.24.64
Ⓗ Arcade

4 rue Maréchal Foch
☎ 38.54.23.11
Ⓗ Berry
1 boulevard de Verdun
☎ 38.54.42.42
Ⓗ Blois
1 avenue de Paris
☎ 38.62.61.61
Ⓗ Central
6 rue d'Avignon
☎ 38.53.93.00
Ⓗ Escale du Port Arthur
205 rue de l'Eglise
☎ 38.76.30.36
Ⓗ Grand Hôtel
1 rue de la Lionne
☎ 38.53.19.79
Ⓗ Marguerite
14 place du vieux marché
☎ 38.53.74.32
Ⓗ Jackotel
18 place du Cloitre Saint Aignan
☎ 38.54.48.48
Ⓗ Le Rivage
635 rue de la Reine Blanche
☎ 38.66.02.93
Ⓗ Saint Jean
19 rue Porte Saint Jean
☎ 38.53.63.32
Ⓗ Saint Martin
52 boulevard A.Martin
☎ 38.62.47.47
Ⓗ Sanotel
16 quai Saint Laurent
☎ 38.54.47.65
Ⓗ Urbis
15 avenue de Paris
☎ 38.73.39.93
Ⓗ Bannier
13 faubourg Bannier
☎ 38.53.25.86
Ⓗ El Castille
57 rue des Carmes
☎ 38.53.39.60
Ⓗ Coligny
80 rue de la gare
☎ 38.53.61.60
Ⓗ l'etoile d'or
25/27 place du vieux marché
☎ 38.53.49.20
Ⓗ Aux Normands
3 rue de la cercle
☎ 38.62.46.91
Ⓗ de Paris
29 faubourg Barnier
☎ 38.53.39.58
Ⓗ De Sonis
46 boulevard de Châteaudun
☎ 38.53.72.36
Ⓗ Touring
142 boulevard de Châteaudun
☎ 38.53.10.51

Ⓗ de Trévise
7 rue Croix de Malte
☎ 38.62.69.06
Ⓗ Charles Sanglier
8 rue Charles Sanglier
☎ 38.53.38.50
Ⓗ Le Paddock
127 rue de la gare
☎ 38.53.39.43
Ⓗ Saint Pierre
60 rue Sainte Catherine
☎ 38.53.38.77
Ⓗ du Sauvage
71 rue de Bourgogne
☎ 38.62.42.31
Ⓗ Campanile
326 rue Chateaubriand
☎ 38.63.58.20

Oravault
Ⓗ Pithiviers
2 rue Robert Chasteland
☎ 40.40.25.06
Ⓗ de l'ancien relais
13 place de l'église
☎ 40.63.01.03
Ⓗ Frank
Route de la Garenne
☎ 40.63.04.79

Oudon
Ⓗ du Port
Place du Port
☎ 40.83.60.09

Pithiviers
◠
2 rue Madeleine roland
☎ 38.30.18.50

Pontchateau
Ⓗ Auberge du Calvaire
☎ 40.01.61.65

Les Ponts de Cé
Ⓗ le Bosquet
2 rue Maurice Berne
☎ 41.57.72.42

Rivarennes
◠ Armentières
☎ 47.27.56.10

Rochefort sur Loire
Ⓗ Grand Hôtel
30 rue René Gasnier
☎ 41.78.70.06

Rochefort
◠ Le Patureau
Mr Georges Blanvillain
☎ 41.78.32.68

🏨 grand Hôtel
route Nationale
☎ 41.92.68.52

Ronceveau
⌂
☎ 64.24.14.04

Les Rosiers sur Loire
🏨 Au Val de Loire
Place Jeanne de Laval
☎ 41.51.80.30

Saint Dyé sur Loire
⌂ Maison de Loire
76 rue Nationale
☎ 54.81.60.46

Sainte Maure de Touraine
⌂ Vallée de Courtineau
☎ 47.27.56.10

Saint Etienne de montluc
🏨 l'escale
rue de la paix
☎ 40.86.86.85

Saint Florent le Vieil
⌂ des Coteaux
☎ 41.72.52.37
🏨 Hostellerie de la Gabelle
12 quai de la Loire
☎ 41.72.50.19

Saint Jean de Braye
🏨 Promotel
☎ 38.53.64.09

Saint lyphard

44410 Herbignac
⌂ "Kerhinet"
Mr Lataste
☎ 40.61.94.06

Saint Pierre de Vaux
⌂
Mr Leroux
☎ 41.51.81.76

Saint Rémy la Varenne
⌂
Mr Jean du Reau
Le bourg
☎ 41.57.02.13

Saumur
⌂ CIS
Rue de Verdun
☎ 41.67.45.00
🏨 Central Hotel
23 rue Daille
☎ 41.51.05.78
🏨 Le Volney
1 rue de Volney
☎ 41.51.09.54
🏨 Le Cristal
10 place de la République
☎ 41.51.09.54

Savenay
🏨 Le chène vert
Place de l'Hôtel de Ville
☎ 40.56.90.16
🏨 L'oisellerie
12 route du lac
☎ 40.56.98.78

Savenières

49170 Saint Georges sur Loire
⌂ La Sellerie de Fresne
☎ 41.72.85.00
or 41.72.21.39

Sennevières
⌂ Le Bourg
☎ 47.94.79.57

Suce sur Erdre
🏨 Au cordon bleu
102 rue de la Mairie
☎ 40.77.71.34

Tours
37000 Tours
🏨 Regina
2 rue Pimbert
☎ 47.05.25.36
🏨 La résidence
12 Place Rabelais
☎ 47.37.03.93
🏨 Le Voltaire
13 rue Voltaire
☎ 47.05.77.51
🏨 Foch
20 rue du Marechal Foch
☎ 47.05.70.59
🏨 de Rosny
19 rue Blaise pascal
☎ 47.05.23.54
🏨 Family
2 rue Traversière
☎ 47.05.25.63

Treves Cunault
49350 Gennes
⌂ La Métairie
Mr Vincent
☎ 41.67.92.43

INDEX

Details of bus/train connections have been provided wherever it was possible. We suggest you refer also to the map inside the front cover.

Amboife 79
🅱 Office de Tourisme,
Quai Gen.-de-Gaulle
☎ 47.57.09.28.
Ancenis 146
🚌 Paris-Nantes
Angellerais (L') 171
🚃 TTO no. 50
Nantes-Savenay (except Sundays and public holidays)
Ardenay 125
Artannes-sur-Indre 91
Au Bignon d'Hoscas 191
Augerville-la-Rivière 27
🚃 S.N.C.F. Montargis-Malesherbes
Aulnay-la-Rivière 30
🚃 Châtelain buses, Orléans-Nemours
Atelier (L') 71
Avaray 63
Azay-le-Rideau 95
🅱 Office de Tourisme, Rue Nationale
☎ 47.45.44.40.

Bagneux 109
Ballan Miré 89
Banque (La) 155
Bas-Retais (Le) 140
Baule 59
Beauchêne 155
🚃 TTO no. 40 Nantes-Laval via Châteaubriant
Beaugency 59
Beaulieu-sur-Layon 133
Beauregard (Château de) 71
Béhuard 123
Bellevue 153
🚃 TAN route 83 Nantes, Haluchère
Besné 177
🚌 1 train daily in each direction (except Saturdays, Sundays and public holidays)
🚃 TTO no. 72 Redon-Saint-Nazaire (except Sundays and public holidays)
Blaison 116
Blois 73, 75
🅱 Office de Tourisme, Pavillon Anne-de-Bretagne, 3 Avenue J.-Laigret
☎ 54.74.06.49.

Bois-Joubert 179
Bondaroy 34
Boulancourt 27
Bouzonville-au-Bois 39
Brainson (Le Bois) 117
Brevets (Les) 147
Briarres-sur-Essonne 28
🚃 S.N.C.F. Montargis-Malesherbes. Châtelain buses, Orléans-Nemours
Brière (La) 177, 178, 192, 195
Brigné-sur-Layon 129
Buthier 24
Buthier Leisure Centre 24

Candé-sur-Beuvron 77
Candes-Saint-Martin 103
Carrefour des Fontaines 41
Cellettes 71
Cellier (Le) 153
🚌 Nantes-Angiers (1 train daily in each direction)
🚃 TTO no. 46 to Nantes; connection at St. Mars-la-Jaille to Châtcaubriant (except Sundays and public holidays)
Chailles 39, 75
Chalonnes-sur-Loire 125, 136
🚌 Angres-Cholet
🅱
Chambord 65
🚃 STD buses, Blois
Champtoceaux 148, 149
Chancelée 71
Chanteloup water tower 35
Chanteloup (Pagoda) 83
Chappelle Notre-Dame-de-Dougarant 167
🚃 No. 6 Saint Nazaire-Horbignac (except Sundays and public holidays)
Chapelle-Saint-Blaise 95
Chapelle-Saint-Mesmin (La) 51
Châteaupaune 139
Chargé 79
Chaumont-sur-Loire 77
🅱
Chaussée (La) 99
Chaussée-le-Comte (La) 69
Chauvigné 116
Chécy 47
🚃 T.R.E.C. route 3 Orléans-Bonney-sur-Loire,

route 6 Orléans-Ferrière-en-Gâtinais, route 11 Orléans-Beausse-la-Rolande, route 14 Orléans-Châtillon-Coligny
🅱
Cheille 95
Chênehutte-les-Tuffeaux 111
Chilleurs-aux-Bois 41
🚃 S.N.C.F. Etampes-Orléans, Orléans-Malesherbes. Châtelain buses Orléans-Nemours
Chinon 99
🅱 Office de Tourisme, 12 Rue Voltaire
☎ 47.93.17.85.
Clermont Halt 151
🚌 Nantes-Augers (1 train daily in each direction)
Clenord 71
Combleux 49
🚃 T.R.E.C. route 11 Orléans-Beaune-la-Rolande
Cour-Cheverny 71
Cour Dieu (La) 43
Courcy-aux-Loges 41
Croix de Coëtquen (La) 185
🚃 TTO no. 20 Nantes-Vannes
Croix Morzel (La) 171
🚌 Nantes-Redon, Nantes-le Croisic
🚃 TTO no. 50 Nantes-Savenay (except Sundays and public holidays)
Cumeray 113
Cunault 112

Dampierre-sur-Loire 105
Deffay (Château de) 177
Denainvilliers (Château de) 37
Denée 121
Domaine de Bois-Joubert 181
Donnery 47
🚃 T.R.E.C. route 11 Orléans-Beaune-la-Rolande. S.N.C.F Orléans-Montargis

Erigné 119
🚃 City and CFIT services to Angers
Escrennes 38

🚍 *S.N.C.F.*
Etampes-Orléans,
Orléans-Malesherbes. Châtelain
buses, Orléans-Nemours.
Estouy 31
🚍 *Châtelain buses,*
Orléans-Nemours

Fay-aux-Loges 45
🚍 *T.R.E.C. route 11,*
Orléans-Beaune-La-Rolande.
S.N.C.F. Orléans-Montargis
Faye d'Anjou 131
Fontrevaud-l'Abbaye 101
🅱 ☎ *41.51.71.21.*
Fossé Neuf (Le) 145
Fourneaux (Les) 53, 146
Francorville Mill 29

Garde (La) 123
Gennes 113
🅱 ☎ *41.51.93.52.*
Goulière (La) 154
🚍 *TTO no. 60 Nantes-Château-Gontier (except Sundays and public holidays)*
Gravelais (La) 185
Guérande 196
🚍 *TTO no. 51 La Baule-Piriac (except Sundays and public holidays), no. 52 Guérande-Mesquer, Guérande-Pompas (Saturdays only)*
Guichetière (La) 145

Haie-Longue (La) 125, 135
Haut des Bruyerès (Forester's lodge) 43
Huisseau-sur-Cosson 69
Husseau-sur-Loire 83

Ingrannes 43

Jubins (Carrefour des) 139
Juigné-sur-Loire 119

Kerhinet 194
Kerbourg 195

Launay 154
Launay (Château de) 129
Lestiou 59
Loge-de-Vallée (La) 145
Louet 121
Lussault-sur-Loire 83

Malesherbes 23
🚌 *Paris-Malesherbes*
🚍 *S.N.C.F.*
Orléans-Malesherbes via Pithiviers,

Montargis-Malesherbes via Briarres-sur-Essonne
🅱 *Office de Tourisme, 2 Rue Pilonne*
☎ *38.34.81.94.*
Mantelon 121
Marcheboire (La) 141
Mardié 47
🚍 *T.R.E.C. route 3 Orléans-Bonny-sur-Loire, route 6 Orléans-Ferrière-en-Gâtinais, route 11 Orléans-Beaune-la-Rolande, route 14 Orléans-Châtillon-Coligny*
Mareau-aux-Bois 39
🚍 *S.N.C.F. Etampes-Orléans, Orléans-Malesherbes. Châtelain buses Orléans-Nemours*
Marillais (Notre-Dame-du) 145
Marson 109
Martigné-Briand 129
Maslives 65
Mauves-sur-Loire 153
🚌 *Nantes-Angers (several trains daily)*
Mer 63
Mesnil Farm 30
Mesnil-en-Vallée 141
Métaire (La) 111
Métaires (Les) 177
Meung-sur-Loire 57
Milly-le-Meugon 127
Mirebou (Moulin de) 23
Mont-près-Chambord 71
Montjean-sur-Loire 139
Montlivaut 65
Montlouis-sur-Loire 83
🅱 ☎ *47.45.00.16.*
Montsoreau 103
🅱
Motte (Ferme de la) 39
Muides-sur-Loire 63
Murs-Erigne 121

Nantes 153
🚍 *TAN route 56 to city centre*
Nantes (La Jonelière) 161
🚍 *TAN route 51 for city centre*
Nantes (Le Petit Port) 161
🚍 *TAN routes 25, 51, 52, 53 and 86*
Naudières (Les) 169
🚍 *TTO no. 20 Nantes-Vannes via la Roche-Bernard (except Sundays and public holidays)*
Neuville-sur-Essonne 30
Norielle (La) 175, 179

Nove des Gâtis (Forester's lodge) 41

Onzain 77
Orléans 50, 51
🅱 *Offiice de Tourisme, Place Albert ler*
☎ *38.53.05.95.*
Orvault 165
🚍 *TAN no. 80 Nantes-Beausséjour, no. 73 Nantes Pont du Cens (connection for city centre). TTO no. 71 Nantes-Guémené Penfao.*
Orville 28
🚍 *S.N.C.F. Montargis-Malesherbes*
Os (Le pont d') 193
Oudon 148
🚌 *Nantes-Angers (1 train daily in each direction)*

Pagerie (La) 113
Parnay 105
Patoche (La) 147
Pigeon Blanc (Le) 191
Pinçon 25
Pithiviers 35
🚍 *C.E.A. uniroute Paris-Aubigny. Châtelain buses Orléans-Nemours. S.N.C.F. Etampes-Pithiviers, Etampes-Orléans, Orleans-Malesherbes*
🅱 *Mail-Ouest Gare Routière*
☎ *38.30.50.02*
Pithiviers-le-Vieil 38
Pommeraye (La) 140
Pont Brûlé (Le) 182
Pont du Cens 165
Pont-de-Ruan 91
Pont-qui-Tremble (Le) 121
Pontchâteau 177
🚌 *Redon, Quimper, Brest, Rennes, Nantes, Paris, Lyon, Bordeaux, Toulouse, Marseilles, Nice, Saint-Nazaire*
🚍 *TTO no. 20 Nantes-Vannes, no. 72 Redon-Saint-Nazaire*
Pressoir (Le) 141
Puiseaux 28,29
🚍 *S.N.C.F. Montargis-Malesherbes. Châtelain buses, Orléans-Nemours*

Rablay-sur-Layon 133
Ranrouet (Château de) 189
Rilly-sur-Loire 77

Rochecorbon 85
🅱
Rochefort-sur-Loire 123
Rochelle (La) 99
Rocher (Le) 177
Rochemenier 129
Roncevau 25
Rue-de-Meneuil 69
▬ STD buses to Blois

Sache 93
Saint-Ay 57
Saint-Aubin-de-Luigne 133
Saint-Benoit-la-Fôret 97
Saint-Dye-sur-Loire 65
Saint-Etienne-de-Montluc 170
📨 Nantes-Redon, Nantes-
le Croisic
▬ TTO no. 50 Nantes-
Savenay (except Sundays and
public holidays)
Saint-Florent-le-Vieil 143
Saint-Georges-des-Sept-Voies 113
Saint-Gervais-La-Fôret 73
Saint-Gregory Grotto 33
Saint-Jean-de-Braye 49
▬ T.R.E.C. route 3
Orléans-Bonny-sur-Loire, route
6, Orléans-Ferrières-en-
Gâtinais, route 1
Orléans-Chatillon-Coligny.
S.E.M.T.A.O. city bus service
Saint-Jean-des Mauvrets 119

Saint-Laurent-du-Mottay 141
Saint Lyphard 191
Saint-Maur Abbey 115
Saint-Pierre-en-Vaux 113
Saint-Remy-la-Varenne 115
Saint-Saturnin 119
Sainte-Reine-de-Bretagne 185
Saumur 105, 107, 109
📨 Tour-Nantes, Saumur-
Thouars, Saumur-La Flèche
🅱 Office de Tourisme,
Place Bilange
☎ 41.51.03.06
Savenay 173
📨 Redon, Quimper, Brest,
Rennes, Nantes, Paris, Lyon,
Bordeaux, Toulouse, Marseilles,
Nice, Saint-Nazaire, le Croisic
▬ TTO no. 20 Nantes-
Vannes, no. 50 Nantes-Savenay,
no. 44
Saint-Nazaire-Châteaubriant
(except Sundays and public
holidays)
Sencie (La) 181
▬ TTO nos. 50 and 53
Nantes-Piriac, Le Croisic via
Saint-Nazaire and La Baule
Souzay-Champigny 105
Suce-sur-Erdre 157
▬ Transports Brodu route
2 Nantes-Grandchamps-des-
Fontaines (except Sundays and

public holidays), TAN route 86
Petit-Port, route 96 Beausejour
(connection for city centre)
Sully-la-Chapelle 45

Télégraphe (Le) 163
▬ TTO route 10 Nantes-
Rennes
Thouaré 153
📨 Nante-Angers
▬ TAN route 92 to Nantes
Thourcé 131
Thoureil 115
Tours 87
🅱
Trelan 186
Trèves 111, 127
Trezan 25
Turquant 103

Vallée (La) 95
Vallée Mabile (Lac de la) 173
Vernon 59
Villaine-les-Rochers 95
Villemolle 111
Villeneuve 129
Villereau 29
▬ Chatelain buses,
Orléans-Nemours
Vouvray 85
🅱

Yèvre-le-Chatel 30